BREATHE AGAIN

REIGNITING YOUR SPIRIT
WITH THE LIFE OF GOD

CHRIS HODGES

THOMAS NELSON
Since 1798

Breathe Again

Published by Thomas Nelson, 501 Nelson Place, Nashville, TN 37214, USA. Thomas Nelson is a registered trademark of HarperCollins Christian Publishing, Inc.

Thomas Nelson titles may be purchased in bulk for educational, business, fundraising, or sales promotional use. For information, please email SpecialMarkets@ThomasNelson.com.

Italics in Scripture quotations reflects the author's emphasis.

ISBN 978-1-4002-5493-4 (audiobook)
ISBN 978-1-4002-5491-0 (ePub)
ISBN 978-1-4002-5415-6 (TP)

HarperCollins Publishers, Macken House, 39/40 Mayor Street Upper, Dublin 1, D01 C9W8, Ireland
(https://www.harpercollins.com)

Library of Congress Cataloging-in-Publication Data

ISBN 978-1-4002-5415-6

Printed in the United States of America

25 26 27 28 29 LBC 5 4 3 2 1

To the amazing people of Church of the Highlands:
So much of this book came from what we experienced together.
You are a breath of fresh air to me.

CONTENTS

PART THREE: FINDING THE SOURCE OF BREATH

INTRODUCTION

Let us then approach God's throne of grace
with confidence, so that we may receive mercy
and find grace to help us in our time of need.

HEBREWS 4:16

Approach often determines ascent.

Pilots know this, as do business leaders and entrepreneurs. I'm convinced that followers of Jesus need to learn it as well. But before I say more about the importance of our spiritual approach, let me offer some personal background.

I first developed and began preaching this message when the church I'd founded was still young. Growth had exceeded our hopes and expectations, and we were starting new campuses as well as ministering in prisons. I was frequently asked to speak and teach at conferences and events, in order to train other pastors and ministry leaders to help their churches and organizations reach their full growth potential. People wanted to know why our church was growing so rapidly and how we maintained our focus.

My best and most concise answer was that we simply tried to be a breath of fresh air. We wanted a life-changing impact on everyone who walked through the doors. We wanted them not only to experience the love of Jesus but to desire the same joy and sense of purpose in their own lives. In speaking, teaching, and writing, I hoped to convey to others the importance of this spiritual ingredient. I wanted everyone to know God personally, to find freedom from the past, to discover their divine purpose, and to make a difference in the world around them.

In the years since, I've learned to emphasize also the necessity of *choosing* your approach toward God. That's something we often overlook—in part because we're conditioned (by our upbringing, family and friends, popular culture, other Christians, and churches we've attended) to settle for religion instead of relationship.

The decision to accept salvation through God's grace and the sacrifice of Jesus on the cross is deeply personal. It's not a box you tick or a bucket list item to check off. This commitment relies on surrendering your life to God and welcoming the gift of his Spirit within you. It's a transformational pivot—*from* who you used to be (relying on your own abilities when facing life's limitations) *to* who God created you to be—his beloved child relying on the Holy Spirit for limitless spiritual strength and power.

This decision radically changes you, but it doesn't mean your life will be easy, comfortable, or free from conflict and challenges. It *does* mean that you now have a relationship with God that empowers you to do what you can't do on your own while facing hardships and struggles. You not only have spiritual resources, including God's Word and prayer; you also have a family of believers supporting, encouraging, and helping you.

The problem, though, is that many followers of Jesus lose sight of their relationship with the Lord and his resources. They take on a performance-based approach that's all about how much they do. And enough is never enough. They stop relating to God internally and start focusing on the external—what others think of them, what they achieve, how smoothly their life rolls along. Rather than delighting in God, they rely on duty—which eventually leads to resentment, anger, disappointment, even rebellion.

So *how you approach God* is foundational. In the pages to come, I refer often to choosing the tree of life rather than the tree of the knowledge of good and evil—two trees that symbolize how we approach God based on the choice given to Adam and Eve. We'll explore this together.

Being intentional about how you approach God allows you to enjoy life abundantly—to experience the joy, peace, and purpose that Jesus came to bring (John 10:10). It's so tempting to look for fulfillment in what we do, what we own, where we go, who we know. Our culture compels us to compare and compete—rather than experiencing our true identity as a beloved child of our Abba Father. By allowing the world and past wounds to filter our view of God, we lose sight of what's true; we easily slip back into performance mode. This directly affects how you respond when life's hurricanes and heartbreaks hit you. Without trusting God through life's dark valleys, we lose sight of his goodness. We succumb to doubt based on our human limitations. When life doesn't make sense, how we view God determines whether we grow closer to him or more distant.

These trials often bring painful losses, unexpected struggles, and traumatic assaults. But even everyday life can leave us feeling stuck in the doldrums—especially in those seasons when doubt, fear, anger, resentment, grief, depression, or anxiety temporarily overwhelm us. We feel adrift, floundering, unable to move forward. Our view of God will then determine whether or not we get derailed.

I've been a pastor for more than forty years. I've seen God bless the church he invited me to start nearly twenty-five years ago with growth and impact to change thousands of lives. I've watched my God-given dream of founding a fully accredited, state-of-the-art ministry training college come to life beyond anything I imagined. And I recently decided to follow God's guidance and shift my primary energies to serving Highlands College. I'm reinvigorated as I pour all I can into helping it have the greatest eternal impact, while still being part of what God is doing at Church of the Highlands as long as I can.

Wherever you are in your relationship with God, I hope this book gives you spiritual refreshment and a second wind as you run the race of faith. We're told that God breathed life into dust to create the first man and woman. So it's no coincidence that when the Holy Spirit descended on early believers at Pentecost (as foretold and promised by Jesus), they felt the rush of a mighty wind. My prayer is that you'll grow more reliant on the Father who loves you and fills you with his Spirit—the ultimate breath of fresh air. May he breathe new life into everything you do.

PART ONE

SEARCHING FOR A BREATH OF FRESH AIR

1

THE DOLDRUMS

We were almost lost in the middle of the Pacific.
We almost capsized in those doldrums.

ROBERT ANDERSON

Most mornings I wake up happy and optimistic, looking forward to another day. I've never been a depressed kind of guy. But in 1999 I had the worst year of my life. On paper everything looked perfect, and there were no external clues pointing to my interior struggle. My wife loved me and our children were healthy. The church where I was an associate pastor was a thriving, growing community of passionate believers. I'd even been doing some consulting for other churches that were interested in using our church as a model for their growth plans. There was money in the bank and the bills were paid. I had friends—both old ones I'd known since high school and new ones in our neighborhood—who genuinely liked me and seemed to care about me.

But I had never felt more miserable.

Despite all the good things in my life, I'd been experiencing new and weighty challenges: difficult relationships that were growing more complicated because of miscommunication and distrust, worries about the future and meeting the financial needs of our expanding family, a stale spiritual life with little desire to spend time in prayer or Scripture, uncertainty about whether I was where God wanted me to be. Was I really cut out to be a pastor? Somehow I just couldn't envision doing the same thing for the rest of my life. But when I thought about it, I wasn't sure *what* I envisioned for the rest of my life.

In the deepest part of me I wondered: *Is this all there is?*

As weeks dragged on, I became mired in a swamp of unpleasant emotions that I wasn't used to feeling—at least not all at once, and not with such increasing intensity. I was deeply sad, but I was unsure why. I sensed anger and frustration, but that was probably because I felt so stuck in my sadness. And then there was the fear.

I had never experienced anything like this, and I didn't know what to make of it.

I hid it as long as I could. I tried to pretend there wasn't a storm cloud constantly roiling inside me, one that seemed only to grow darker, with more thunder rumblings and lightning strikes of acute emotion. That storm never broke; it continued to gather itself over and over again inside my mind and heart.

I knew I was depressed but hated to admit it, even to myself. I'd never experienced such depression before, and I'd even been quietly critical of those who seemed to fight an ongoing battle with it. I always thought, *Just choose to be happy and get on with your life, buddy!* Those thoughts now mocked me because I wasn't sure how to change what I felt inside. I couldn't pinpoint exactly what my feelings were, but I knew I couldn't change them simply by telling myself, *Don't worry, be happy.*

I wasn't sure if the problem was spiritual or physical, mental or emotional, or all the above. So I did what so many of us do: I forced myself to go through the motions. At church staff meetings, I acted like I couldn't be happier, nodding and smiling, detached from the storm inside me. I'd go home and try to act normal. If my wife Tammy or our kids mentioned that I seemed to be discouraged, I dismissed their comments with, "I'm okay—just tired."

This went on for months. Then in January of 2000, our church focused on a prayer effort called "21 Days of Prayer," a time of personal fasting, prayer, and listening for God in our lives. Everyone was asked to participate at whatever level they felt led. This was the fourth time our church had started the year this way, and I'd always been involved, although not very seriously.

But this time I was so desperate to hear from God that I went to extremes. Figuring the new year might be my opportunity for a fresh start, I went on a complete fast: no food, no media, no distractions. I would pray and read only my Bible. I was determined to give this a shot, and I committed to going to the doctor afterward if this time alone with God didn't reveal what was going on. (I probably should have gone already, but my stubborn ego kept thinking I could handle it.)

Then on day seventeen of my fast, God visited me during one of the morning prayer services at our church, as I was worshiping and seeking him in prayer. I'll never forget that moment. It remains one of the seminal events of my entire life. His presence was so real, his voice so clear, that the storm inside me broke. Like the sensation of a cool, refreshing rain on a hot summer day, his presence revived me. I also received a picture in my heart, an image of me leading a congregation of people. I had an open vision of myself preaching in a large auditorium before more than two thousand people. I could see their faces, and I immediately knew I cared for them, though I hadn't even met them yet.

Until that point, I'd never even considered being a senior or lead pastor. In my seventeen years of ministry, I'd wanted only to be the best number two guy on the planet. Yet God spoke to my heart and said that he would lead me to something that year—and it would be my assignment for the rest of my life.

TURNING POINT

Now this vision may not sound like much, but it gave me tremendous hope. Shortly after the fast was over, I met with my pastor, Larry Stockstill, and learned that God had spoken to him too. Larry said it was time for me to launch out and lead a church of my own, and he wanted to help me. From then on, one door opened after another, and God made it clear what path he wanted me to follow. I quickly became more passionate, more excited, and more alive than I'd ever been. And I know I would never have gotten there if not for experiencing that year in the doldrums.

God used that time of desperation and depression to get my attention in the most dramatic way possible. Apparently, it often takes something painful—sometimes even tragic—to get us to listen to God. But that time of prayer and fasting was like a breath of fresh air. The fast disconnected me from the world, and my prayer time connected me to God. Looking back, I suspect God was talking all along and I just couldn't hear him. Somehow I had sensed this and become very sad that I was missing out on the huge heart message he wanted to give me. My depression forced me to stop and listen.

Today, I'm founding pastor of one of the largest congregations in the country, a dynamic, life-giving church that I love. I've often thought that I wouldn't even be a pastor here in Birmingham, Alabama, if I hadn't gone through that difficult time of feeling stuck. I had to find a way to move through it and allow God's breath to fill my sails.

Maybe you struggle with depression or have gone through a season like the one I described. You might even feel like you're going through the motions right now, unsure of what's wrong but definitely sure that something's not right. Perhaps the hardest part is that your faith feels thin and flimsy, unable to bear whatever it is that's rumbling deep inside you.

Maybe you grew up in the church and know all the right things to say and do. Or maybe religion was not a part of your upbringing—you or your parents didn't see any real joy in the lives of those people who claimed to be filled with the love of Jesus. Or maybe you've experienced this kind of going-through-the-motions numbness in other areas of your life. At work. In your marriage. With your kids. In your friendships. You're waiting for something to happen, for the storm inside you to break, for a fresh breeze to breathe new life into you. You're not sure how to make it happen. But you know there has to be more.

THERE HAS TO BE MORE

There's something amazing about feeling a warm ocean breeze across your face from the deck of a ship. And watching the wind fill a giant piece of canvas, tilting that large sail in a way that both powers and directs the vessel, is even more incredible. Before the age of motorized boats, merchants, explorers, and sailors relied on these trade winds to carry them to certain places, especially across the ocean to another country or continent. You've probably seen enough Pirates of the Caribbean movies to know this, even if you haven't been out on a sailboat yourself.

Prior to the twentieth century, however, all mariners knew about one area that was to be avoided at all costs: the Doldrums. Taken from the root word meaning "dull" or "lifeless," the expression "in the doldrums" was used to describe the state of being bored and restless, in a slump. Sailors then gave this name to a specific region along the equator where the weather always seemed to illustrate this lifeless condition.

Because of the way the earth rotates, the currents and clouds of the Northern Hemisphere literally collide with the winds and weather of the Southern Hemisphere, creating an area of unpredictable weather. Usually extending between five degrees latitude north and five degrees latitude south of the equator, the Doldrums are also known as the Intertropical Convergence Zone (ITCZ).

Normal trade winds converge in this band along the equator and basically cancel each other out, creating a still, windless dead zone. Their collision also produces convectional storms that result in some of the world's heaviest precipitation. Since there's no wind to move them along, just an air mass hovering overhead, these storms keep sailing ships stuck in place.

It's not surprising, then, that the Doldrums were once feared more than the Bermuda Triangle. Many ships became trapped in the dead zone, forced to endure grueling storms until they wrecked. Sailors would try everything they knew to do to get the ship sailing again, but usually nothing worked. They were stuck, sometimes permanently.

While our GPS systems and hydraulic engine technology now protect ships from the dangers of the equatorial Doldrums, its emotional equivalent seems more prevalent than ever. We still use this figure of speech to describe someone who's in a slump, listless, despondent, stagnant, and going through the motions. I can't think of a better word to describe what I experienced in my church growing up, then later as a young adult when I found myself caught back in a spiritual performance trap.

I think most of us can relate to being in the doldrums. You may know what you're supposed to do in life, you may even know where you want to go, but you are stuck in this zone where there's no wind, no breath, no life, nothing to help motivate you and move you along. Maybe you're going through a storm and doing all you can just to stay afloat. Maybe it's been a long time since you've been fired up about anything. Maybe you're in a rut and don't know how to move forward.

There's usually no single reason for you to feel immobilized like this. Like cool air colliding with tropical winds over the ocean, your doldrums may be the result of a number of factors converging. Nonetheless, it's usually helpful to think about what has contributed to your present location in life. Let's quickly look at some reasons you may find yourself stuck in the doldrums.

DRIFT AWAY

Have you ever spent a lazy day at the beach, riding the waves and bodysurfing? I love doing this with our kids, but it's always amazing where we find ourselves after we've been out in the water for an hour or two. We look back at the shore and suddenly nothing looks familiar. We can't see our umbrella or beach chairs—sometimes we can't even see our hotel! Without realizing it, we have drifted with the current and lost our bearings.

Without a strong direction toward a place where God is moving, without a secure anchor to keep you grounded, it's easy to drift into a dead zone. You may be doing all the right things—at home, at work, at church—but you don't know where your life is headed. You feel lost and disoriented from where you thought you'd be and how you thought you'd get there. But it's almost too terrifying to acknowledge, so you just keep going with the flow day after day.

When I was reading about the Doldrums that sailors face, I was struck by the fact that this dangerous dead zone happens along the equator. When ships got trapped there, it meant they weren't really in the Northern Hemisphere or the Southern Hemisphere; they were stuck where the two meet. I think we often get stuck in a similar manner. If we're being honest with ourselves, we know we don't want to go to hell, yet we don't really want to serve God either. We want to have one foot in the world and the other in the kingdom of God. We want to straddle the spiritual equator, so to speak.

A lot of us have drifted to this place. We're not on fire for God, but we're not living for the devil either. We're not abandoning God and leaving the church, but we're not fully alive and enjoying the abundant life Jesus said he came to bring. We're in this middle zone, a spiritual no-man's-land.

We have gotten off course, and now there's no wind to sustain us. This isn't a new phenomenon. In Revelation 3:15–16, Jesus essentially tells the church at Laodicea, "Some of you are not hot (you're not in the Northern Hemisphere); you aren't even cold (you're not in the Southern Hemisphere); you're lukewarm." And the result is just as disastrous: "There's no life there. I'll spit you out of my mouth, if I find you in that lukewarm zone."

In his letter to the church at Corinth, Paul conveyed a similar message. He told them that he could not consider them spiritual, but he could not call them worldly either. They were a mixture of the two. They were "carnal" (as we see in 1 Corinthians 3:1 KJV). The word *carnal* means they were stuck in the flesh. The word's root comes through in a usage you may be more familiar with: chili con carne—chili with meat. Paul basically said these Corinthian Christians were serving up a big dish of faith con carne. They were Christians but still had some flesh-based living in them.

Many of us today follow the same recipe. We want enough Jesus to get us to heaven, but we've got a little bit of the world in us too. We're lukewarm, tepid, not hot or cold, not heavenly and not earthly, not sold out to God and not entirely through renting from the devil. So we drift away and get stuck in the doldrums.

EYE OF THE STORM

Sometimes we don't drift into the spiritual doldrums but are pushed there by life's disturbances. In fact, the doldrums are a magnet for life's storms. The storms will either get us there and keep us there, or else they will happen while we're there. A huge part of the problem is that most of us don't respond to storms correctly. Instead of running to God for shelter and protection, we run from him, usually right into the eye of the storm.

When the storm winds are blowing and life gets hard, many people feel like they've done something wrong—perhaps even something to deserve their present crisis—and therefore they stay away from God. After all, he'll only punish them more, right? Or when times get hard, they seem to think that God hasn't kept his end of the bargain. They went to church, prayed, read their Bibles, served those around them—and now this is how God repays them? They feel like they did everything they were supposed to do and had the right to expect that God would prevent trials from happening in their lives.

So we get stuck in the doldrums and may even come to view ourselves as victims. No matter what happens, we always seem to be heading into another storm. Maybe it's losing our job or watching our retirement fund shrink to less than where it started. Maybe it's an ongoing illness or injury, if not our own then that of our kids or someone else we love. It could be that our marriage has lost its passion and now we feel stuck in a lifeless relationship. How are we supposed to cope with any one of these crises, let alone the perfect storm that occurs when they collide?

For some people, the answer becomes a secret addiction, a way of numbing the pain by finding a few fleeting moments of pleasure. It could be alcohol or prescription drugs, shopping and then shopping some more, watching porn and withdrawing from our spouse, chatting with a sympathetic stranger online, or staying busy with work 24–7.

We try anything to keep ourselves from thinking about the storms in which we find ourselves—anything to ease the pain. And yet these attempts to gain relief only create more storms as we come to rely on our addictions. Once again, we discover that we are unable to move.

LOSING OUR BALANCE

So often, doldrums are the result of weariness and spiritual fatigue. Like a sailor with no compass and no sense of direction, we find ourselves aimlessly following others' wishes, having lost the ability to say no. We don't want to disappoint anyone, right? So we try to do it all—to be the supermom or the perfect dad; to climb the corporate ladder; to lead the Bible study; to head up the kids' fundraising drive; to stay on top of household chores.

The result? We burn out and become cynical, angry, frustrated, and soul weary. Our marriages, which started out so beautifully, now seem more like an arrangement of convenience in which two roommates share possessions and custody of the kids. We secretly resent and withdraw from each other. The job that energized our careers and brought us such excitement now comes at us like a double-decker bus, one that we seem to get thrown under by everyone at the office.

People who were once our friends now really annoy us because it seems like they always want something from us. They rant on and on about their problems, never once asking how *we* are doing. The kids seem only to need more and more while saying thank you less and less. More chauffeuring, more money, more help with homework. And if it's not the kids needing us, it's our own parents, becoming more and more reliant on our help as they age.

We feel there's no one to talk to, no one who understands how much responsibility we carry. We're so unbearably lonely, even when dozens of people are around. We bury our emotions below the surface because we're afraid that if we release them, they'll overwhelm us and we'll never function again. We've lost our sense of balance and now neglect the basics. In fact, we've lost not only our sense of balance in life but also our sense of purpose. The joy of knowing who we are and what God created us to do seems like a distant memory at best.

We're burned out, weary to the bone, scared, and anxious—and there's no end in sight. The doldrums spin us round and round, and we don't know which way is up. God doesn't seem to care enough to do anything about where we are. So we carry our pain alone and try to keep going for one more day.

JUST BE IT

Being stuck in the doldrums reminds me of a time when Tammy and I were vacationing with friends and we decided to go snorkeling. We're experienced swimmers and love the water, so we couldn't wait to see all the brightly colored varieties of fish and aquatic life awaiting us below the surface. We were especially excited when our guide told us he'd saved the best locale for last: an underwater cave we could swim through.

He explained that we would pop down a foot or so below the surface, enter the mouth of the cave, see some amazing species of exotic fish, and come out the other side to resurface. Because of the direction of the current, we could not turn around and come out the way we entered, so we needed to keep moving forward to exit the shallow cave. It sounded easy enough, and we couldn't wait.

Down I popped below the surface, with my wife and one of our friends following. I swam through the craggy mouth of the reef-like tunnel and marveled at the way sunlight sparkled through eroded holes in the cave's ceiling, spotlighting the way ahead. But as I kicked forward, I realized the cave extended longer than I expected—much longer. Finally, I could see the murky light of the exit, but it appeared so far away.

I was already out of breath and knew my snorkel tube wouldn't work below the surface. There was no way I could fight the current and turn around. Kicking harder and harder, I swam as fast as I could and began to wonder if I was going to make it.

Although I wasn't in deep water, I felt claustrophobic and tried to resist panicking. Was this how I would die? I knew people could drown in shallow water just as easily as in deep. And how about Tammy and our friend behind me? Where were they? Were they okay?

Finally, I reached the end, forced my body through the rocky exit, and surfaced. It was tighter than the entrance had been, and I scraped my back and shoulders coming up. Still, I was so glad to breathe again! It took another couple of minutes before Tammy finally surfaced, gasping and bleeding after cutting her back on the rocky exit even worse than I had. Our friend made it out too. But all of us were done for the day. What had started as a fun excursion became a death-defying experience that left us exhausted and more than a little relieved to have made it out.

The doldrums often affect us in a similar way. We find ourselves in a storm or just in a rut, and suddenly we think we'd better try harder. If only we'd exercise more, stay later at the office, help out with the household chores more, spend more quality time with the kids, pray more often, read the Bible every day . . . well, then everything would be all right. But of course we only end up burned out and on the brink of spiritual, physical, and emotional exhaustion.

The doldrums flourish when we're focused on *doing* rather than *being*. We forget that real life happens internally more than externally. We would rather *do* something than *be* something.

There are always two ways to determine behavior—by internal motivation and by external motivation. In other words, every behavior is motivated either by an internal force or an external force. I can drive at a safe speed out of concern for my safety and the safety of the people around me, or I can do it because of the highway sign telling me I have to drive at a certain speed. I can be faithful to my wife out of love for her, or I can be faithful in obedience to the biblical law that says, "Thou shalt not commit adultery." I believe there's a constant tension in us and in our society between internal motivation and the use of external constraints to determine our behavior.

It's always much easier to have an external rule to make us behave. But while rules are important, that's not the gospel. The good news that Jesus brought is about a transformation of the inner person that makes us different at our core.

If you're ever going to make it out of the doldrums—and stay out—it comes back to your inner motivation. *Why* do you do what you do? What are you wanting to do with your life? Where do you want to go?

This book's purpose is to put wind in your sails again. To get you unstuck. To move you through the storm. To help you reclaim your compass and redirect your course. Heaven knows, we don't need another motivational, inspirational, feel-good self-help book. I'm not saying that these books aren't helpful or even biblically based—just that there are already plenty of them. Most of them focus on changing behaviors and cultivating habits. Again, that's not necessarily bad; it's just inadequate for making lasting change.

You can focus on externals all you want and try to imitate the methods of others in hopes of duplicating their success, purpose, or happiness. But you'll only end up on the treadmill of disappointment, more frustrated than before, unless you make changes on the inside first.

If you want a rush-of-grace breath of fresh air in your life that will resuscitate your spirit and bring you closer to God—and closer to being the person he made you to be—this book is for you. I'm convinced that if you pursue God, you'll experience a passion and zeal for living while enjoying every dimension of your life as never before. You'll discover the X factor—that rare, life-giving quality that we'll explore further in the next chapter—and it will manifest itself in everything you do.

We'll also look at some of the practices that everyone knows are important, but few have learned to implement in a life-giving way. And every one of them, when practiced in that life-giving way, will draw you closer to God and out of the doldrums. Although these practices are not in themselves the secret to a changed life, I believe they're a means to access the power that can change yours.

Yes, it will require some changes, some discipline, and some perseverance. But if you stick with it, you'll never again have to worry about remaining stuck in the doldrums.

BREATHING LESSON

Perhaps you haven't sensed a fresh breath in your life for a long time. You may have gotten out of touch with the way God is active and moving in your world. If so, you may have difficulty even pin-pointing the cause or determining the route back into the open air.

If you find yourself in the doldrums today, my hope is that this book will refresh you. I want to encourage you to invite God to come alongside you and begin to revitalize you with his healing wind.

And be encouraged. As painful as the doldrums are, God will use this stuck place to do a great work in you. Be assured, when something is happening *to* you, God wants to do something *in* you.

> We were crushed and overwhelmed beyond our ability to endure, and we thought we would never live through it. In fact, we expected to die. But as a result, we stopped relying

on ourselves and learned to rely only on God, who raises the dead. And he did rescue us from mortal danger, and he will rescue us again. We have placed our confidence in him, and he will continue to rescue us.

—2 Corinthians 1:8–10 NLT

2

CATCH YOUR BREATH

Joy delights in joy.

WILLIAM SHAKESPEARE

As a pastor, I've become pretty good at reading people's faces, especially right after a church service. I was once shaking people's hands at the door when a middle-aged woman approached with a scowling face. I was already thinking, *She must've had a bad experience.* She looked me in the eye. "Well, Pastor, I've found something I don't like about this church."

I kept smiling, pretending I wasn't discouraged to hear this. I confess I'd already started thinking bad thoughts even as I said, "Tell me what you don't like." Her face instantly changed. Her scowl became a smile—she'd been messing with me the whole time! "The one thing I don't like, she said, "is that I have to wait six more days before I can come back!"

She went on to tell me how she'd attended church her whole

life but never enjoyed it until she found our church. She teared up a little as she described how going to church was now something she did out of delight, not duty. I asked her what this difference felt like, and she answered, "It's like a breath of fresh air. It's like I can breathe again. This church has taken my relationship with God from the *got to* to the *get to*."

FRESH BREATH

The apostle Paul, who regularly endured hostility and persecution, had ample reason to be in the doldrums. In the midst of such difficulty, how did Paul find an environment that was both life-giving and life-changing?

In a little-known passage, Paul described one particular friend as one who "refreshed" him. His name was Onesiphorus, one of those behind-the-scenes guys you may never have heard of. The Greek word Paul used to describe him literally means "to put breath back in, to recover breath." It's as if Onesiphorus gave Paul emotional CPR, breathing encouragement and inspiration into his Christian brother. "May the Lord bless Onesiphorus and all his family because he visited me and encouraged me often. His visits revived me like a *breath of fresh air*" (2 Timothy 1:16 TLB).

Maybe you have a friend who always manages to cheer you on, someone who offers support in tangible ways. I've been blessed to have more than one such friend. One in particular stands out—my father-in-law. Although Billy passed away more than a dozen years ago, his impact on my life endures.

Billy counseled me in a way that always made me feel stronger, smarter, and more talented than I felt before I approached him. I could rest in his friendship. I came to depend on time with him to recharge my batteries and renew my spirit.

People like Onesiphorus and Billy tend to have enormous impact in subtle ways. With enthusiasm, positive approach, and energy for loving others, they breathe life into those around them and transform the environment. Even if you haven't experienced this kind of relationship firsthand, we've all sensed the difference between a place with fresh air and a place without it. Sometimes you notice it as you walk into a room; other times, it doesn't reveal itself until after a few visits. But there's definitely some quality in these people and their attitudes that can make any environment a magnetic, life-giving, enjoyable place to be.

THE X FACTOR

In a classroom, we sense immediately if the teacher is fueled by a life-giving undercurrent of passion—or they're uninterested in both the subject matter and the students they're teaching. The students can be the same, the room the same, textbooks and assignments the same. But the teacher makes the difference between an engaging, exciting, you-love-being-there kind of class and a lifeless, boring, you-can't-stay-awake kind of class.

At the office, it's the difference between an environment where everyone watches the clock and feels stifled and weary, and one where time flies, with everyone enjoying what they're doing and feeling committed to working together as a team. It's the quality you see in the dedication and enjoyment people have in their roles, the spark in their eyes that shows they truly can't wait to get out of bed in the morning and go to work. Usually there's a boss or supervisor who loves working with people, and whose positive attitude becomes contagious.

You also recognize this life-giving quality quickly in some people's homes. We've all been in small starter homes that overflowed with warmth and charm, and in luxurious mansions that were as cold and lifeless as a concrete slab. The people inside, of course, provide the unique quality that transforms a house into a home—with a welcoming, inviting, relaxing environment that makes you feel special, like you belong.

When a church has this life-giving factor, you sense it within the first visit. There's something different about the atmosphere. People are truly glad you're there and naturally eager to get to know you. They demonstrate compassion and humility and a genuine commitment to serve others. They display a shared bond in strong friendships, life-giving marriages, and healthy families. The people respect and accept and serve one another, and simply enjoy worshiping and being together. There's a shared commitment to similar values, and an anchor of confident security in their faith. You want some of what they have!

Not long ago someone sent me a blog post written by Audrey, a member of one of our campuses. Audrey describes the intangible quality that she and her husband noticed the first time they came to the church. I think she explains it just about as well as I ever could:

> The minute I walked into the building something felt different . . . something actually felt right. People were packed like sardines in the sanctuary—standing room only—and these people were freely worshiping God through song and praise. The Holy Spirit blanketed this room and I could feel him . . . this must be home.[1]

Audrey and her husband, Chris, quickly connected with a pastor and became members of the church and one of our small groups. They wanted more of this refreshing breeze—and they now contribute to this fresh-air environment themselves.

This mysterious factor feels like the heartbeat of a relationship, a home, a business, a classroom, a church. It feels like a breath of fresh air, an energy-giving, life-breathing force that draws you in and inspires you, empowering you to be all that God made you to be. You know when it's there and you know when it's not. But what is it? More importantly, how can you get it?

You've likely experienced this mysterious quality at one time or another. You may link it to certain kinds of people and places, but it's usually hard to pin down. It's an intangible force that inspires you with energy and fills you with new breath. It causes you to grow in ways you could never achieve by yourself.

While it may manifest in many different ways, this element emerges from your approach to God—from how you view him and relate to him, and how this motivates all you do for him.

The Bible begins (in Genesis 1–3) by describing God's acts of creation, then focusing on a life-changing choice facing Adam and Eve. Having been made in the image of their divine Creator, the first man and first woman were given free will, the ability to choose how they would relate to God. They were given two options, represented by the tree of life and the tree of the knowledge of good and evil, with each resulting in profound consequences.

We're no longer in the garden of Eden, but we face the same choice in how we relate to God. We can choose the tree of life and experience its abundant, life-giving, dynamic eternal fruit. Or we can choose the tree of the knowledge of good and evil and harvest its scarce, life-draining, bitter earthly fruit.

With the contrast between them so clear, I doubt few of us would consciously choose to settle for anything less than the tree of life. And yet so many people who long for a spiritual breath of fresh air overlook how they connect to their Source.

BRANDING PROBLEM

On one occasion years ago, I was flying home from a pastors' conference in Louisiana. The flight to Birmingham was full. No sooner had I settled into my window seat than I looked up to see a young woman boarding who might have just stepped off Bourbon Street. Laughing and high-fiving as if entering a party with old friends rather than a flight with strangers, she made a beeline for the seat next to me. We exchanged pleasantries and she introduced herself as Tanya.

Once we were airborne, she waited until she had a drink in hand from the refreshment cart before asking me the inevitable question every pastor dreads in these situations: "So what do you do for a living?"

I told her I was a pastor.

"Duh," she responded, "we're all passengers."

"No," I said. "A *pastor*—like at a church."

"Well, I don't like Christians."

Having anticipated something like this, I immediately said, "I don't like them either. At least, not the kind I'm guessing you're talking about." This was clearly not the response she expected.

"I thought you had to like 'em," she said.

"I don't like people who believe that Christianity is something it's not," I explained. "Which is why I think Christianity has a branding problem. Being a Christian is not about your denomination, or church, or organization. And it's not about following all the rules and doing everything right. Christianity is about your relationship with God."

Tanya rolled her eyes and lifted her drink toward me, spilling a little in the process. "So what does God think of *this*?"

I smiled and said, "I don't think he cares much at all about it. He cares about *you*!"

My response surprised her, just as it often catches many people off guard—including those who consider themselves believers. The problem is that too often we relate to God based on assumptions and false notions we've picked up from other sources—our family, friends, church experiences, and cultural stereotypes—rather than discovering the true Source for ourselves.

How you relate to God is foundational to how you view yourself and others. Your approach to God determines whether you live in freedom or in a performance mindset.

Don't take my word for it—consider what God's Word says about it. After the creation account in the Bible's opening chapter, the narrative that immediately follows focuses on the choice all human beings face about how we approach and relate to God:

> Now the Lord God had planted a garden in the east, in Eden; and there he put the man he had formed. The Lord God made all kinds of trees grow out of the ground—trees that were pleasing to the eye and good for food. In the middle of the garden were the tree of life and the tree of the knowledge of good and evil. (Genesis 2:8–9)

The story progresses logically enough, with God creating a home for his human creation—a beautiful place that would also produce food. We're specifically told that God made all kinds of trees, but our attention falls on two in particular: the tree of life and the tree of the knowledge of good and evil. After God tells the man to work and tend the garden, he adds this warning:

> You are free to eat from any tree in the garden; but you must not eat from the tree of the knowledge of good and evil, for when you eat from it you will certainly die. (2:16–17)

Just as these two trees are literal as well as symbolic, I believe God's warning extends beyond physical death. It also works metaphorically: Eating from the tree of the knowledge of good and evil leads to the death of your efforts, your dreams, your goals, and your relationships.

Note also that choosing to eat from this tree includes knowing good as well as evil. This is not simply an either-or choice between good and bad, obedience and rebelliousness, God and not God. It's bigger than that. We choose either a transforming of our heart, or striving for external behaviors. Because God desires relationship with us, not just compliant behavior, the tree we choose determines our worldview and our God-view.

SEEDS OF DOUBT

God gives us this choice, just as he did with Adam and Eve. Meanwhile, the enemy looks for any opportunity to play mind games that pull us away from trusting God. Notice his strategy in the garden (which he also pursues with us today):

> Now the serpent was more crafty than any of the wild animals the LORD God had made. He said to the woman, "Did God really say, 'You must not eat from any tree in the garden'?"
>
> The woman said to the serpent, "We may eat fruit from the trees in the garden, but God did say, 'You must not eat fruit from the tree that is in the middle of the garden, and you must not touch it, or you will die.'"
>
> "You will not certainly die," the serpent said to the woman. "For God knows that when you eat from it your eyes will be opened, and you will be like God, knowing good and evil." (3:1–5)

The devil wasted no time in planting seeds of doubt in her mind—the realm of knowledge. The enemy began by challenging the truth of what God tells us: "Did God really say . . . ?" (3:1). The serpent insinuated that God's message and motive were not only inaccurate but intentionally deceptive. Deception is never God's method. But the devil, as the "father of lies" (John 8:44), relies on it repeatedly.

Once doubt was planted, the serpent proceeded to contradict the truth God had spoken. He told Eve and Adam that they would *not* die, but would in fact become just like God—with their eyes opened to knowing good and evil. Notice again that the fruit of this tree is not entirely evil but good as well, indicating that we can do good things for the wrong reasons. This is the essence of a performance-based faith. We try to know God and please him based on what we do rather than how we relate to him.

This is an ongoing temptation when we rely on our own knowledge instead of on the new life we have in our relationship with God. We're told that Eve and Adam made a choice that seemed logical enough based on the knowledge at hand. The fruit of the tree of the knowledge of good and evil looked appetizing, and based on what the serpent told them, it would also gain them divine wisdom.

After choosing to disobey God's instruction, they ate the fruit (Genesis 3:6-7), and their eyes were indeed opened—resulting not in their becoming God-like, but mired in shame. Aware of their own nakedness for the first time, Adam and Eve created something to hide behind: fig-leaf garments to cover up their mistake. We follow their example when we live in our own knowledge rather than in God's grace. We go our own way, experience shame, and try to hide.

DUTY OR DELIGHT

Let's dig deeper and compare these two trees to see the contrast in how we approach God based on our choices.

Perhaps the greatest difference is in what each tree tells us to *do*. The tree of the knowledge of good and evil insists, "Do more to get to God." The implication is that we must work harder to assuage his anger. This reflects what I call the "Wizard of Oz" view of God—seeing him as great and powerful but also fearful and transactional, just like the Wizard in the classic tale. When Dorothy tells him she wants to go home to Kansas, the Wizard requires that she first bring him the broom of the Wicked Witch. When we have this view of God, we assume we'd better do what he tells us in order to get what we want.

But the tree of life tells us, "Jesus has already done it." There's nothing we must do to receive God's love, grace, and forgiveness and to experience life as his beloved child and co-heir with Christ.

Jesus's death on the cross paid the debt we could never pay ourselves, so we can live in freedom from performing and trying to live up to the law. In the Pharisees, we see this performance mindset being confronted by Jesus: "You study the Scriptures diligently because you think that in them you have eternal life. These are the very Scriptures that testify about me, yet you refuse to come to me to have life" (John 5:39–40).

The Pharisees followed this approach: "Keep trying to get God's approval." This is what many Christians still believe today. They assume God is angry and out to condemn them for the many ways they fall short in thoughts, attitudes, and actions. They view God as a curmudgeonly judge with a huge club waiting to punish them. They regard him with fear, anxiety, anger, and resentment. Once again, the way you view God determines how you approach him. If you assume he's harsh and unforgiving, that will control how you relate to him.

But in the tree of life's message, this truth is found: "He already loves you." On your worst day, in your most shameful moments, God loves you just as much as when you're walking with him and obeying his Word. He may not like what you do when you go your own way and choose to sin, but he always loves you just the same.

As a parent of five grown children, I love my kids even when they mess up. I can recall times when they messed up royally; I didn't like what they had done, but my love for them never wavered. I remember telling them, "You have never needed me more than you do right now. You can't handle this situation alone, and you don't have to—that's why I'm your daddy."

God loves us so much more than any human parent loves their children. He loves us so much that he gave up his most precious and only Son to sacrifice himself in order for us to have relationship with him for eternity. Which is why my favorite Bible verse has always been Romans 5:8—"But God demonstrates his own love for us in this: While we were still sinners, Christ died for us."

The tree of the knowledge of good and evil says, "Obey God out of duty"; the tree of life says, "Obey God out of delight." Duty views the Bible as just a rule book, a repeating series of "You must do this" and "You'd better *not* do that"—which once again tilts us into performance mode. But delight views the Bible as God's gracious guidance for how to know and love him.

Obeying out of duty, we'll never get it right all the time. We'll check boxes, try harder, spend more time in prayer and Bible study while watching the clock. And we'll become resentful, angry, and even bitter as we realize we can never do enough to sustain God's favor.

Fortunately, we need do nothing to earn God's favor! The tree of life draws us into a loving, intimate relationship with our Abba Father, with his Spirit dwelling within us. When know and love him this way, the temptation to look elsewhere for life or to rely on our own efforts will fade. We're assured that "this is love for God: to keep his commands"—because when we're motivated by delight, we know that "his commands are not burdensome" (1 John 5:3).

DEEP-ROOTED RELATIONSHIP

So how do we live in the tree of life, not the tree of the knowledge of good and evil? We do it by focusing on our choices and how they color the way we perceive and approach God. We cultivate a deep-rooted relationship with the living God. We fall in love with Jesus—which may sound easier said than done. But remember, falling in love is effortless when we have the right view of God.

Jesus told his followers, "If you love me, keep my commands" (John 14:15). Too often we assume he meant that we have to keep his commands in order to be loved by him. But the truth is that when we fall in love with him, we keep his commands automatically. We fulfill the commands of the Bible better by falling in love with God rather than trying to obey everything the Bible says.

Staying grounded in the tree of life also means you serve God through relationship and not rules. This is the crucial difference defining the Old and New Testaments. The Old Testament focused on external compliance to laws written on tablets. The New Testament maintains those laws but with a radically different approach to keeping them. Thanks to Jesus's sacrifice on the cross and the gift of the Holy Spirit, the focus has shifted to our internal relationship with God. Jesus said, "Do not think that I have come to abolish the Law or the Prophets; I have not come to abolish them but to fulfill them" (Matthew 5:17). This shift means we respond to all sin by remembering the truth symbolized by the tree of life.

Although we're saved by grace and in relationship with God, we all still sin at times, and we face a choice in how we handle our mistakes. When we go our own way instead of God's, we can easily give way to the lie of condemnation—that we're no good and unworthy of God's love when we mess up. *Or* we can believe what's actually true: We messed up, but God has given us a way forward.

We see this illustrated vividly in the encounter between Jesus and the woman caught in adultery, which we read about in John 8:1–11. The Pharisees and Jewish religious leaders thought they'd finally cornered Jesus with an inescapable trap. The law stated that the punishment for adultery was death by stoning, so Jesus could either endorse this woman's murder for her sin, or else let her live and thereby break the law.

Instead of falling for their trap, Jesus balanced grace with truth. He told the onlookers that whichever of them had never sinned should throw the first stone. Those religious leaders began to slip away one by one. Finally, no one was left—only Jesus and the woman. He asked her, "Where are your accusers? Didn't even one of them condemn you?" When the woman replied that none remained to accuse her, Jesus said, "Neither do I. Go and sin no more" (John 8:10–11 TLB). He showed grace by refusing to condemn her, even as he maintained the truth by telling her to leave her sinful ways.

This is the transformative tension we're called to maintain as we live in the freedom of the tree of life. We guard our hearts from slipping back into the old performance mindset based on externals, and remain in the freedom of our identity in Christ. It's an ongoing daily process in which we recognize the choice before us: "This day I call the heavens and the earth as witnesses against you that I have set before you life and death, blessings and curses. Now choose life, so that you and your children may live" (Deuteronomy 30:19).

CATCH THE BREEZE

I'm convinced that all of us are capable of living in the freedom represented by the tree of life. That's what this book is all about. Maybe you've been in the doldrums or are going through a slump in your life. Maybe you find yourself in a life-draining crisis, or more likely, you're just numb from going through the day in, day out routine of life. You get up, get the kids ready for school, go to work, chauffeur kids around for sports, go home, have dinner, clean up, look over a report for work, pay the bills—and finally collapse exhausted into bed so you can do it all over again tomorrow.

Maybe there's some variety on days when you work overtime, or meet with your small group from church. But it all blurs together. You wonder why you do what you do. You don't stop and step back and look closely at your life, for fear of what you'll find. You don't even know if you're happy, or if you're doing what you should be doing. You simply exist.

Our journey together in these pages is about reclaiming your life and breathing fresh air into all of it. You may feel like you're gasping for air, needing CPR. Or maybe you're at the top of your game, and like an elite athlete on the sidelines, you simply need refreshment before you reenter the competition.

Most likely you alternate between those feelings. Some days you feel on the verge of a breakdown; other days, a short breather is all you need. Either way, we all long for that sweet sensation of allowing a gentle breeze to caress us. Whether we're in the doldrums, in a hurricane, or in calm waters—you and I need wind in our sails to move forward.

The strategies in this book go beyond "seven principles to a happier life." They're not more ideas on how to be a better Christian, or guidelines for controlling your behavior. The internal combustion of personal passion requires something supernatural happening inside you. It requires God's grace-rushing presence in a real, tangible, feel-it-everyday kind of way. Which means falling in love with him—with who he really is—like never before.

BREATHING LESSON

The apostle Paul wrote Timothy about the friend who had refreshed him like a "breath of fresh air." If you long for your own Onesiphorus, begin to pay close attention to the source of any cool refreshing breezes currently blowing in your life. As you do, you'll discover it's relatively easy to spot the difference between a person or place that pours life into you, and those that drain you.

When did you most recently notice a person or place that brought you a breath of fresh air? How did this refresh you? Once you're able to recognize the intangible qualities that invigorate you, you'll find it easier to pursue their sources.

> Today I have given you the choice between life and death, between blessings and curses. Now I call on heaven and earth to witness the choice you make. Oh, that you would choose life, so that you and your descendants might live!
>
> —Deuteronomy 30:19 NLT

3

DO YOU LOVE ME?

God loves us the way we are,
but too much to leave us that way.

LEIGHTON FORD

Like a lot of people in the Deep South, I grew up going to church every time the doors were open. I don't think I ever missed a Sunday in my life—ever. In addition to the two services on Sunday, my family also attended every Wednesday night prayer meeting. But the Sunday morning services are what I remember best. My dad, the church organist, played the three-keyboard Wurlitzer on the right-hand side of the platform across from the pianist, Mr. McCutcheon, who was seated to the left of the pulpit. In her burgundy choir robe, Mom sang soprano in the church choir, which consisted of a couple dozen members.

From these vantage points, both my parents could keep their eyes on my siblings and me during the service. Sure, we whispered and giggled and pinched each other and chewed the gum that my grandmother would give us (even though Dad didn't like it), but we were always aware that if we got too loud (signaled by Dad looking over his shoulder in our direction), there was going to be some serious discussion when we got home.

Just because I spent all that time in church didn't mean I necessarily liked it. I knew it was probably good for me, like running wind sprints in gym class or eating brussels sprouts. But I assumed that meant I wasn't supposed to enjoy it. It was just what you did if you were a good family in Baton Rouge back in the seventies.

RELATIONSHIP, NOT RELIGION

I never doubted God's existence or the need to trust Jesus to save me. As I got older, I prayed and read my Bible, and I often responded to the altar call at the end of the service. But even though I tried to learn more about God and the Bible and what Christians were supposed to do, I always felt that no matter how much time I put in, it was never going to be enough. Every time I went to church, I either heard about the things I shouldn't be doing that I was doing, or I heard about the things I wasn't doing and needed to do.

This was the only approach I knew to having a relationship with God. I tried to please him by doing the right things and by not doing the wrong things. Sometimes I wondered if it was even worth it.

The truth is, I really didn't like church—and I didn't enjoy many Christians. While they smiled, nodded, prayed, and said, "God bless you, brother," my impression was that they seemed just as frustrated as I was underneath their good church faces. It was probably because they didn't want to be there either. Or at least that was my theory.

I had so many questions. Why was it such a struggle to do everything right? How could I actually enjoy this so-called wonderful, joy-filled Christian life? And why, despite all my efforts to do everything right on the outside, did I still feel so empty, numb, and lifeless on the inside?

Since then I've discovered that when the focus is on doing spiritual things and avoiding sinful things, the motivation is all wrong.

That realization happened in my sophomore year of high school. By the time I turned fifteen, I had secretly checked out on God but still attended church every Sunday and went through the motions. Then a friend of mine invited me to a youth service at his church. The worship there was like nothing I'd ever seen before. In some strange way, I was both attracted to it and scared to death at the same time. People seemed genuinely happy and excited, and they passionately praised and worshiped God. Not only that, but the youth pastor taught in a way that I understood and that seemed relevant to my everyday life.

I'd never seen young people so in love with God. I couldn't believe it! This was so different than anything I'd ever experienced. I asked myself, *Is this real? Or is this some kind of cult? If this is who God really is, then I want to know him, love him, and follow him for the rest of my life.*

When I got home I opened my Bible, determined to discover for myself what it really meant to be a Christian. I'm thankful the church I was raised in taught me enough about the Bible that I could search the Scriptures for myself.

I started with the Gospels, opening to the book of Matthew, and began reading. My goal was simple: Find out what the Bible says about how a person gets to heaven. And then it happened. The verses in Matthew 7 jumped off the page and answered my question—and it was completely different from anything I'd ever heard before!

> Not everyone who says to me, "Lord, Lord," will enter the kingdom of heaven, but only the one who does the will of my Father who is in heaven. Many will say to me on that day, "Lord, Lord, did we not prophesy in your name and in your name drive out demons and in your name perform many miracles?" Then I will tell them plainly, "*I never knew you*. Away from me, you evildoers!" (Matthew 7:21–23)

For the first time I realized that God wasn't keeping a checklist, marking down what I was doing and not doing. He just wanted to *know* me. My eternal destiny wasn't about religion but relationship. And so on that December night in 1978—Christmas break of my sophomore year of high school—I gave my life to Jesus and told him that if he would give me another chance, he would never find another person who would follow him with more passion than I would. It may sound clichéd, but truly, that night my life changed forever.

Five years later, at the age of twenty, I wound up on staff at the same church I had visited with my friend. After that December night, I'd fallen in love with God and committed myself to him. I wanted to serve him, and it made sense to do it at the place where I first experienced such an alive, dynamic faith.

However, as I grew in my relationship with God and served in ministry, I discovered that I had a tendency to fall right back into the same spiritual numbness I'd felt before my conversion experience.

When Tammy and I were still fairly new parents, I was serving as a youth pastor in Colorado Springs. Every morning I spent time in my little office in our basement, reading my Bible and praying. One morning after about a half hour down there, I heard Michael's and Sarah's footsteps as they ran squealing across the kitchen just above me. Their laughing voices made me want to run upstairs and join the fun.

Right then I got real honest with my heavenly Father. "God, I don't want to be down here right now. This is work, and I'd rather be upstairs playing with my kids. Why is that?"

I sensed God's voice telling me, "Because your relationship with them is different from the one you have with me."

"Lord, what do you mean?" I asked.

"You treat me so formal—everything timed, everything out of obligation. And You don't talk to me the same way you talk to them. What would it look like if you talked to me like you talk to them? What would it be like if you were just in love with me?"

It's difficult to describe the weight that was lifted off me once again. God was reminding me that I could either try to get closer to him by doing the right things and hoping it would "take" on the inside, or I could fall in love with him on the inside, knowing that everything would then happen naturally on the outside.

There seems to be something in our human nature that draws us away from a life-giving relationship with Jesus because it feels more comfortable to focus on what to do and not do. That tendency robs us of real joy and peace. As a young pastor trying to live up to people's expectations, I had fallen back into the pattern of trying too hard to do everything perfectly—which of course I couldn't do.

INSIDE OUT

I'm not alone in this struggle. Many people are still trying to reach God through religion. They're doing everything right on the outside but remaining empty on the inside. Maybe you're in the same boat—caught in the doldrums of wanting more and not knowing how to move forward. Here are a couple of indicators that you need some fresh air in your life.

Symptom number one is that you're doing the right things but you don't enjoy them. This feeling goes beyond simple fatigue or occasional boredom to indifference. A subtle, unspoken sense of "What difference does this make?" creeps in. You may even feel a little guilty for not having the peace and joy that you once experienced, or that you've heard someone who's in love with God should experience.

Another classic symptom is when you begin to envy others who seem to grow closer to God, although what they're doing seems no different than what you're doing. Doing the right thing seems to be working for everyone but you. As you look around at the people in your church or in your group of Christian friends, you notice that their efforts seem to be producing fruit where yours never have. You read the same books, go to the same small group, even do the same Bible studies, and yet your attempts remain dry, lifeless, uninteresting, and uninspiring.

This isn't just a twenty-first-century American phenomenon. In every nation of the world and in every period of time, you'll find people practicing liturgies, reciting prayers, and obeying traditions while their hearts are far from God. They desperately try to know God by doing the right things externally. But perhaps the problem is more prevalent in our world today. In our technologically advanced age, where every problem has a solution, every bad habit can be changed, and every flaw can be corrected, we still cannot reduce our relationship with God to a formula.

We get stuck in a mindset that tells us that what we do on the outside is the end in itself. Don't get me wrong—it's good to do good things. We can't rely on our feelings as the engine to fuel our actions, just like a musician can't wait until she has inspiration to play, but must develop her talent by practicing every day. It's the internal motivation, the passion fueling our desire, that determines whether or not our endeavor has breath.

But how can we tap into this spiritual passion within? How can we cultivate our relationship with God and not get caught up in the performance trap of religion?

LOVE RULES

Answering this question has been mankind's struggle since the garden of Eden. From the very beginning of creation, people have always been given a choice. With Adam and Eve in the garden, it was whether to eat from the tree of life or from the tree of the knowledge of good and evil. Would they choose the fresh air of relationship with their Creator? Or the performance-only trap of external dead works?

We know what they chose and the chain reaction it set off for all humankind. But why did Adam and Eve make that choice? And why do we so often follow their example? I believe it's because we think it's easier to measure, to quantify, and to control our behavior when we have an external set of rules. When we have a checklist to work from, we can track our progress and know where we stand. Besides, relationships are messy.

And yet relationships are what we're made for, what we all crave on the inside. Most religious people are banking their salvation on what they do right and avoid doing wrong. As long as their behavior conforms to this standard, they figure they're in the clear. They feel they deserve to know God's favor, live a prosperous and joyful life, and go to heaven when they die. After all, they've done everything right, haven't they?

Probably one of the most surprising discoveries I've made while studying the Bible is that God does not condone religion. It's a consistent theme throughout Scripture. Religion is man's external effort to please God. But God doesn't care about all my efforts to get those things right. He wants more—something far greater.

In fact, this is one of the main issues Jesus confronted while on earth. He ignited a huge explosion within the religious establishment because he came and said, "I'm the Messiah, the Son of God. And you know what? Religion isn't the way to God."

THE CLASH

Most people think Jesus came to bring about a religious order. Throughout history, people of all faiths have called Jesus a religious leader. I think he would have considered that description an insult.

Some of the strongest, harshest language Jesus ever used was aimed at the Pharisees and Sadducees, the Jewish religious leaders of his day. As we look at one of his confrontations with them, I think you'll see clearly that what God wants from them—and from us—is something much more than just obedience:

> Then some Pharisees and teachers of the law came to Jesus from Jerusalem and asked, "Why do your disciples break the tradition of the elders? They don't wash their hands before they eat!" Jesus replied, "And why do you break the command of God for the

> sake of your tradition? . . . You nullify the word of God for the sake of your tradition. You hypocrites! Isaiah was right when he prophesied about you: 'These people honor me with their lips, but their hearts are far from me. They worship me in vain; their teachings are merely human rules.'" (Matthew 15:1–9)

Here it's clear that clean or unclean has nothing to do with germs and aloe-enriched hand sanitizer! The fundamental conflict was about what qualified a person to approach God. For the Pharisees, it was a matter of keeping their own external tradition of washing hands before they ate a meal. But Jesus quickly jumped to the heart of the matter—literally.

He responded to their superficial question about conformity with a profoundly unsettling question about their heart motives. And for reinforcement, he referenced one of their own sources—Isaiah, a prophet they honored. It seems that long before Jesus was born and began his ministry, people had decided they could give God lip service and remain just as self-centered and rebellious as they wanted on the inside.

Instead of focusing on knowing and loving God, their method became a matter of making and conforming to rules. They set themselves up to determine what was and wasn't holy and pleasing to God, often based on their own prejudices and self-righteous judgments. They could feel superior about keeping all the rules they'd made while condemning others who weren't doing the same. Their reliance on external regulations and obligations defined religion. God was kept at arm's length, or rather at heart's length, because they created their own rules.

When Jesus came along and clashed with the religious establishment, he was engaging in a battle that continues today. As I see it, the crucial question comes down to this: How can we get to God? Or to back up a bit, how can we really know God? The way we know him is through worship—opening our hearts to him with honesty, sincerity, and humility. Jesus makes it clear that worship is relational, an internal posture of the heart, not a mechanical pose we can strike just for the sake of appearances. Others may not see the difference, but God knows our hearts and clearly knows the difference.

I DON'T KNOW YOU

Not only was Jesus direct in his confrontation with the religious establishment, he also reinforced the religion-relationship distinction in his teachings. He knew many people approached God through rules rather than relationship, banking their salvation on what they did rather than on who they knew. Understanding that sometimes the truth is more powerful when it sneaks up on us, Jesus often taught in parables—simple stories of illustration that continue to intrigue us today:

> At that time the kingdom of heaven will be like ten virgins who took their lamps and went out to meet the bridegroom. Five of them were foolish and five were wise. The foolish ones took their lamps but did not take any oil with them. The wise ones, however, took oil in jars along with their lamps. The bridegroom was a long time in coming, and they all became drowsy and fell asleep.
>
> At midnight the cry rang out: "Here's the bridegroom! Come out to meet him!"

> Then all the virgins woke up and trimmed their lamps. The foolish ones said to the wise, "Give us some of your oil; our lamps are going out."
>
> "No," they replied, "there may not be enough for both us and you. Instead, go to those who sell oil and buy some for yourselves."
>
> But while they were on their way to buy the oil, the bridegroom arrived. The virgins who were ready went in with him to the wedding banquet. And the door was shut.
>
> Later the others also came. "Lord, Lord" they said, "open the door for us!"
>
> But he replied, "Truly I tell you, I don't know you." (Matthew 25:1–12)

Notice that all the young women were virgins, which symbolizes their religious purity. Also notice that the foolish ones thought that the condition for eternal life was making sure they had done enough—that they had saved enough oil to light their path to go out and meet the bridegroom, a common wedding custom at the time. However, by relying on the issue of how much oil they had in their lamps, they missed the party!

The reason the foolish virgins can't come in has nothing to do with virginity or having enough oil. The bridegroom—representing Jesus himself—doesn't say, "Sorry, your lamps aren't lit, so you can't come in." Nor does he say, "Whoops, I can only admit virgins, and I'm not sure you qualify." No, the reason he gives for not letting them enter is simple: "I don't know you." It's a matter of intimacy, an internal matter of what's going on inside their hearts. All of heaven will be about our relationship with God, not our religion—those things we do on our own to try to gain his favor.

FORWARD MOTION

Maybe you already know the Lord, but the way you know him isn't working for you. You're not enjoying your relationship with him. Here's the real secret: You can fulfill the commands of the Bible better by falling in love with God than by trying to obey him. It's not that your obedience isn't significant or relevant; it's simply not the center of the wheel. The real hub of your life is your relationship with God. Your behavior and obedience radiate like spokes from the center of your life and allow you to roll forward. When you try to make your external behavior the hub on which you turn, you get stuck. Forward motion must be fueled by love.

Some people try to be good by doing godly things—reading their Bibles, praying, and serving those in need. But they're doing these things out of a sense of religious duty and obligation, not because they're in love with God and want to know him and offer up their lives to him. Then they wonder why their spiritual lives are so dry. Aren't they doing everything a good Christian should do? Well, then, why isn't God coming through with his end of the deal? Why isn't he answering their prayers and giving them the abundant life of peace and joy that Jesus said he brought to us?

The Christian faith is not a business transaction. It's not an arranged marriage where you receive a dowry of riches for compliance. Christianity works only if you're in love.

If you're trying to fight temptations by working on self-control, you're working on the wrong thing. I'm all for living a disciplined life, but there's a better way. Temptation is a test of your *relationship*, not your self-control. Whether or not you pray does not depend on your self-control. It does, however, reveal your relationship with God. Do you really want to talk to God? And better still, do you want to listen and hear what he wants to say to you?

It's time to stop trying to please him and simply start loving him. Stop doing things out of obligation. Only do the things that enhance your relationship with him, the things that please you because they delight him.

It's funny, the things we do for love. I hate cleaning out the garage—the time, the effort, the trouble. Sure, the outcome is nice, but is that really how I want to spend a weekend? However, my wife feels like the most loved woman in the world when I help her clean out the garage or tackle some other big project that needs doing. It's better than sending her a dozen roses—well, almost. The point is, I do it because I love her so much—and it brings me joy to do something I know she really appreciates.

What we do for God also reveals the extent of our love. Jesus said, "*If you love me*, keep my commands" (John 14:15). For years I read that verse this way: "If you love me, you will obey me and prove how much you love me." But that's not what Jesus says. He simply says that when we love him, our obedience to him will flow out of our relationship.

I'm afraid most of us don't grasp the enormous extravagance of our Father's love and the lengths to which he's willing to go to show it. That's why the apostle Paul prayed (in Ephesians 3:14–21) that we might know and understand God's love.

One of my greatest revelations of God's love came when my firstborn son, Michael, was about two years old. My wife was attending a friend's baby shower and had taken Michael with her. She was sitting in a metal folding chair and didn't realize that Michael was hanging on the back of it. When she got up, Michael fell backward and pulled the chair right on top of him. The metal chair hit him on the bridge of his nose and cut it wide open. Minutes later, I got the call that my wife and son were on the way to the emergency room.

As the plastic surgeon began to sew up my son's nose, Michael screamed, "Daddy, please—help me, Daddy!" All I could do was watch as the surgeon finished his work. I would have done anything to take my son's place on that table.

On the way home from the hospital, while Michael slept in his car seat, I cried uncontrollably. And in that moment, God spoke to me: "That's the way it felt for me when my Son was on the cross—but I let it happen because I love you, Chris." I realized then how great the Father's love is for me. The fact that he allowed his Son to go through such pain for me—and for you—is overwhelming.

DO YOU LOVE ME?

I've been struck by what it means to have love—rather than tradition, obligation, or manipulation—at the center of your relationship with someone. Channel surfing one night, I caught an old favorite, the musical *Fiddler on the Roof.* I remember seeing it in high school and enjoying the insight into Jewish life and customs and the way the story depicted the clash between tradition and change.

You might recall that the story is about the five daughters of Tevye, a traditional Jewish patriarch, and his wife Golde. Set in Russia at the dawn of the twentieth century, the story explains the custom of allowing a matchmaker to pair an unmarried young Jewish woman with a desirable husband. As Tevye's daughters rebel against this practice and insist on marrying for love, Tevye must wrestle not only with tradition, but also with a far more personal crisis.

Tevye and Golde have been married for over twenty-five years, and like everyone else they know, their wedding was arranged by a matchmaker. In light of their daughters' revolt in the name of love, Tevye asks his wife a crucial question in the song "Do You Love Me?" At first, Golde dismisses his question as silly. After all, she points out, hasn't she always done everything he's ever asked of her? Hasn't she been a good wife?

But Tevye explains that there's a difference between submission based on traditional obligation and submission based on simply loving someone for who they are. Once Tevye makes the distinction clear for her, Golde admits that she does indeed love him, even if such love was not what first brought them together. Their relationship illustrates the contrast between religion and relationship with God in a beautiful way.

Falling in love with God is just like falling in love with another person. You think about him constantly and want to be with him all the time. You can throw away your checklist of what you're looking for in a relationship and just enjoy spending time together. Your only desire is to be with him, to enjoy him, to receive what he wants to give you, and to give him everything you have. Like Tevye's song to Golde, I believe God continues to whisper to each one of us: "Do you love me?"

SHOW YOUR LOVE

It's no wonder so many people don't enjoy their Christian faith when all they know is obligation and duty-motivated obedience. If you're serious about catching the refreshing breeze of God and moving forward, you have to keep your love for God alive. Don't just try to keep it on life support by relying on your religion. That will keep you rooted in the tree of the knowledge of good and evil—and grounded in the doldrums.

Jesus offers you something far better. He invites you to experience him for yourself, to discover who he really is and not just who others say he is. Then we can easily share in what David proclaimed to the Lord: "You are the giver of life. Your light lets us enjoy life" (Psalm 36:9 NCV). That is the key to finding ultimate fulfillment in life. Foster your relationship with God in a way that cultivates and deepens your intimacy. Fall more in love with him. Discover more of who he is. Enjoy the fullness of who he is as your Lord, your Father, your Creator. This is the fundamental message of the Bible—yet I often fear that so many have missed it.

People end up viewing Christians as indentured servants to a divine tyrant who demands good behavior from his followers. Again, they get a negative impression of what it means to have faith in a loving God. They don't see us enjoying a divine romance. Instead they often interpret what they see as something negative or even abusive. But God is the essence of love, the reason we can even attempt to love others. If we ever stop loving God, then it's all over—"Because no one can eat or enjoy life without him" (Ecclesiastes 2:25 NCV).

God invites us into the masterpiece of his love, his character, and his personality directly. It's the key to our ultimate fulfillment in life. Rather than trying to obey a checklist, when we cultivate a relationship with God it's no big deal to obey his commands. We want to please him, to know him, to trust him.

In chapter 1, we exposed the lifeless condition we all can find ourselves in from time to time. And in chapter 2, we explored the refreshing reality of something far better. But before we can experience that process of breathing again, it's critical to realize that it all begins with a vibrant, intimate relationship with God.

Over the years, I've watched discouraged believers—myself included—finally experience the rush of fresh wind that pushed them out of the doldrums when they addressed one or more of the eight areas we'll look at in part two. Each of these attitudes and actions has the potential either to draw us closer to God or move us away from him.

I hope you're convinced by now that a breath of fresh air doesn't come by changing anything on the outside. It doesn't come from formulas, systems, or structures. It comes when something happens inside us—when our love for God is so vibrant, it spills over into the way we see everything.

Discovering love at the heart of our relationship with God breathes new life into every area of our lives, beginning with our perspective and outlook. This is what we'll explore in the chapters to come.

BREATHING LESSON

The Christian faith is not an impersonal business transaction. And Christianity will breathe life into you only if you have an intimate, personal relationship with God. While there are life-giving approaches you can take to grow closer to God (as we'll see in coming chapters), your motivation has to be a desire for relationship, not a sense of duty. You can fulfill the commands of the Bible better by falling in love with God than by trying to obey a checklist of rules.

The question is simple: *Are you in love with God?* Just like Tevye in *Fiddler on the Roof*, God is asking you, "Do you love me?" I encourage you to respond to his great love today.

Start by having an honest conversation with God. Tell him

how you feel and where you're frustrated or afraid of loving him. Spend at least a few minutes listening for his response, perhaps while reflecting on this passage:

> Christ will make his home in your hearts as you trust in him. Your roots will grow down into God's love and keep you strong. And may you have the power to understand, as all God's people should, how wide, how long, how high, and how deep his love is. May you experience the love of Christ, though it is too great to understand fully. Then you will be made complete with all the fullness of life and power that comes from God.
>
> —Ephesians 3:17–19 NLT

PART TWO

BRINGING FRESH AIR INTO YOUR LIFE

4

EYES ON THE ETERNAL

You can't take it with you,
but you can send it on ahead.

RANDY ALCORN

At Christmastime, I've always loved buying presents for my kids, especially when they were young. I would get so excited trying to find a special present for each one of them—something not on their list, something that reflected their unique personality and personal interests.

Some selections were easier than others. My youngest son, Joseph, loved anything remote-controlled—cars, planes, robots, you name it. One year I was traveling home from Sydney, Australia, right before Christmas and saw something in the airport that I knew Joseph would absolutely love. Outside one of the shops, a guy stood demonstrating a remote-controlled toy helicopter. It flew with amazing precision, darting above our heads, swooping down, and zooming back and forth throughout the terminal.

The salesman saw me watching and asked if I wanted to try the remote. I held my hand above my head, palm up, and said, "Put it right here!" He smiled and sent the helicopter in my direction but took the long way. Back into the store and back out again, up above the escalators, then back toward me—where it hovered directly overhead before coming to a perfect landing on my palm.

Needless to say, I was hooked. The copter cost way more than I wanted to pay, but I was so excited thinking about Joseph playing with it that I didn't mind. Truth be told, I was looking forward to playing with it myself!

Now, buying Christmas presents for kids is always a risk. There's the risk that you're more excited about the gift than they are. There's nothing worse than watching them open the box, look up, and give you a courtesy smile before quickly setting your gift aside and moving on to the next package. Or spending an enormous amount of money on their gift only to find them having more fun playing with the box it came in.

I was pretty confident that I had a gift that would not receive either of those responses. And, sure enough, when Joseph opened my present, he was shocked and elated. He ran over and hugged me like it was the best gift he'd ever received. Score one for Dad! He loved it so much that he couldn't wait to get it out and try it. "Gently, gently," I cautioned as he ripped into the box to retrieve it. With the remote loaded with new batteries, he ran out the door with me not far behind. I told him to make sure he was in the middle of our cul-de-sac before starting the copter's inaugural flight—I even made him repeat my instructions back to me.

Within two seconds—his feet were barely out the door—the helicopter not only had liftoff but was stuck on top of our house.

I'm not much of a fix-it guy and didn't even have an extension ladder to climb up on the roof. So I grabbed a fishing pole from the garage in hopes that I could hook the helicopter and lower it down. Well, I hooked it all right—then proceeded to drag it to the edge of the roof, where the rotor blades caught on the gutter and abruptly snapped into pieces. Its maiden voyage was its last, and we were so disappointed.

WHAT DO YOU EXPECT?

Sometimes we're so excited about something in our lives that there's no way it can live up to our expectations.

Like my Christmas day disappointment, have you ever built up your expectations only to discover that things didn't work out the way you had hoped? There's nothing like unfulfilled expectations to take the wind out of your sails. Or as Scripture puts it, "Hope deferred makes the heart sick, but a longing fulfilled is a tree of life" (Proverbs 13:12). When you expect something and envision it a certain way, only to discover it's not that way at all, it really does feel like your heart becomes sick. But if you ever find something real and substantial, something solid that fulfills you inside—it lives and breathes and grows just like a tree of life.

For most of us, however, it's easier to become cynical and quietly desperate as our hope dries up with each unmet expectation in life. We end up feeling powerless to change ourselves, our circumstances, or other people. We hate ourselves for even wanting more or daring to hope that we might get what we long for. Unfortunately, even when we get what we wanted, it's never enough.

King Solomon, the son who followed in his famous father David's footsteps, was perhaps the most successful man who ever lived. He was world-renowned for his incredible wisdom, and he had enormous wealth and a thousand wives.

Even though he thought those things would bring him fulfillment, all of it became meaningless to him. It even brought him to a place of depression and hating his life:

> I denied myself nothing my eyes desired; I refused my heart no pleasure. My heart took delight in all my labor, and this was the reward for all my toil. Yet when I surveyed all that my hands had done and what I had toiled to achieve, everything was meaningless, a chasing after the wind; nothing was gained under the sun. . . . So I hated life, because the work that is done under the sun was grievous to me. All of it is meaningless, a chasing after the wind. (Ecclesiastes 2:10–11,17)

The book of Ecclesiastes describes an unfulfilled life with raw honesty. I'm convinced that it's one of the most relevant, practical books in the Bible for us today. Like Solomon, we often find ourselves in the midst of incredible abundance—a good family, a nice home, a great job, plenty of food and drink, and more clothes than we'll ever wear. And yet, we still find ourselves in the doldrums, stuck in place, going through the motions, and uncertain about how to break free to an authentic life filled with joy and purpose.

One of the reasons I find Ecclesiastes so comforting is that it gives voice to our feelings and describes the barriers that seem to lock us in place and prevent us from experiencing fulfillment in life. Right off the bat, Solomon expresses his frustration in a way many of us can relate to at the end of a long workday:

> "Everything is meaningless . . . completely meaningless!" What do people get for all their hard work under the sun? . . . The earth never changes. (Ecclesiastes 1:2–4 NLT)

Some days it feels like nothing we do matters. And if nothing matters, why bother? Why even make the effort?

Of course, everyone has days like that. I feel that way, at least briefly, just about every Monday. Thinking back over our services the day before, I'm bound to ask myself, *Now why did I say that?* or *Why did I put that song there?* Then there are the times when I've been in the middle of a message series on parenting—at a time when my own teenager isn't speaking to me. Those are typical job hazards of a pastor, I guess. Yet if I focus only on what I and those around me can see, I can get moored in the doldrums pretty fast.

When we experience enough of these days, they begin to have a cumulative effect on our souls. We feel like we're on a treadmill with no hope of getting off and moving forward:

> The sun rises and the sun sets. . . . The wind blows. . . . Around and around it goes, blowing in circles. Rivers run into the sea. . . . Then the water returns again to the rivers and flows out again to the sea. Everything is wearisome beyond description. (Ecclesiastes 1:5–8 NLT)

The cycle seems to continue, over and over again, with nothing changing as we go through the motions of each season. Too often life just wears us out, and no amount of sleep can relieve the weariness we carry inside.

At such times, nothing seems to bring much relief anymore,

not sleep or new clothes or another vacation. We experience the law of diminishing returns. What we hoped would bring us joy isn't cutting it anymore. "No matter how much we see, we are never satisfied; no matter how much we hear, we are not content. History merely repeats itself" (Ecclesiastes 1:8–9 TLB). We feel trapped in the lives we've chosen, contained by the sum of our choices in life. The old saying "Be careful what you wish for—you might get it" stings us with the reality that our lives feel empty even after we have all that we thought we wanted.

DON'T LOSE HEART

While it's comforting on one level to have Solomon articulate our worries and offer a rant that's as timely as any blog entry today, we're still left feeling stuck.

For the substance of real hope that we long for, I believe we must look at someone whose life contrasts with Solomon's in almost every way.

The apostle Paul was at the opposite end of the social, economic, and political spectrum from his poetic predecessor, yet he was clearly far more fulfilled in his life. With no real personal possessions, certainly no permanent home or accumulated wealth, Paul thrived in the windblast of God's Spirit and sailed the adventure of a lifetime. Shipwrecked and imprisoned, beaten and belittled, the guy never lost sight of his first love, and this passionate commitment grounded him regardless of his circumstances. He wrote:

> Therefore we do not lose heart. Though outwardly we are wasting away, yet inwardly we are being renewed day by day. For our light and momentary troubles are achieving for us an eternal glory that far outweighs them all. So we fix our eyes not on what is seen, but on what is unseen, since what is seen is temporary, but what is unseen is eternal. (2 Corinthians 4:16–18)

Paul never lost heart. And neither should we. Why? Because what we see and experience around us is not all there is.

Solomon grasped at all the pleasures the world offered and ended up in despair. Paul tossed aside everything he possessed in favor of loving Christ and ended up with eternal riches—and an appreciation for God's master plan.

At the beginning of this book, I shared my struggle with depression during a watershed year for me and my faith. Even when I was on vacation or engaged in one of my favorite hobbies, I'd often ask myself, *Really? Is this it?* Then God answered in a very real and personal way. He showed me what's real, and he reminded me that what we can see is indeed not all there is. In fact, there's so much more!

After that year ended and I had moved on, I developed what I call my "problems theory" about the way life works. It's pretty simple actually. My theory is that our problems never go away. If you or I solve one, another just pops up in its place. Like dandelions in your yard—or those Whac-A-Mole games at carnivals—one problem is resolved just as another one pops up. You find the money to pay for the car repairs, then the fridge goes out. You finally get the job transfer you've wanted for years, then the company starts downsizing. As Solomon observed, there always seems to be something waiting to undermine our contentment.

THE NEXT BIG THING

That leads me to the conclusion of my theory: If we want to enjoy life in the vibrant, fully alive way that we all crave, we must have something to focus on that is bigger than our problems. When we have a larger perspective, we realize our problems are not very significant in the long run. Ten years from now, are we going to remember why we're mad at our best friend, or how much it cost to pay the late fee on this month's mortgage payment?

And if our problems are far bigger and more life-consuming than those examples, we have all the more reason to recognize that God and his purposes are bigger. When we get diagnosed with cancer or lose our job or get divorced or have sick kids, we wonder how we'll get through it. The only way is to fix our eyes on something beyond our pain.

Once again, I look to the apostle Paul to show us how to do this. He wrote 2 Corinthians after going through many trials in Ephesus. He touched on those trials in this letter's first chapter:

> We think you ought to know, dear brothers and sisters, about the trouble we went through in the province of Asia. We were crushed and overwhelmed beyond our ability to endure, and we thought we would never live through it. In fact, we expected to die. (2 Corinthians 1:8–9 NLT)

If anyone had a reason to wallow in his problems, it would seem to be Paul, who was staring death in the face. Yet he was able to look beyond his troubles. He continued:

> But as a result, we stopped relying on ourselves and learned to rely only on God, who raises the dead. And he did rescue us from mortal danger, and he will rescue us again. We have placed our confidence in him, and he will continue to rescue us. And you are helping us by praying for us. Then many people will give thanks because God has graciously answered so many prayers for our safety. (2 Corinthians 1:9–11 NLT)

Paul was focusing on what was happening *in* him, not *to* him. Likewise, we can be sure that when something is happening to us, God is doing something in us—something that will shape us for eternity.

When my daughter Sarah was a toddler, it didn't take much for her to cry. She was a sensitive little girl, so it was sometimes hard to gauge the seriousness of what had happened based on her response to it. One day she came in crying very loudly and dramatically, and I came running. She'd scraped her knee. Other than being a little red, her knee seemed okay, but she just kept sobbing.

So I comforted her, put a Band-Aid on the hurt knee, and wiped away her tears, only to see them replaced by more. Then, inspired, I went over to our cookie jar and pulled out an orange Tootsie Pop. Sarah immediately stopped crying and directed her attention toward the treat in my hand. Something had come into view that was bigger than her pain.

In the same way, the secret to living life with wind in your sails is to focus on more than your own problems and pain. Regardless of what's going on around you, look beyond yourself. Fix your eyes on the eternal—in every area of your life. What are you looking at when you think about where you are in your life right now? Could it be that your problems are not your real problem? Maybe you just have the wrong focus.

Maybe you're expecting from this life what can only come from God. Maybe you're expecting to receive from other people what only God can give. Maybe you're expecting possessions and experiences to fulfill you in deep ways that only God can touch.

You and I need to get our focus off this life, off what we receive from other people, beyond what we own or see in front of us. We must constantly remind ourselves that the only things that matter are eternal things. The secret of life is to keep our focus there.

This truth leads then to a question: How do we live so that our focus remains on eternity?

EYES ON THE PRIZE

Paul encouraged us to take a different position from the one most of us usually choose:

> Since, then, you have been raised with Christ, set your hearts on things above, where Christ is, seated at the right hand of God. Set your minds on things above, not on earthly things. (Colossians 3:1–2)

Paul exhorted us to look up with both our hearts and our minds so we can see beyond "earthly things" and focus instead on "things above."

Too many times we pray and basically try to bring God down to earth to do our bidding. It's kind of funny, really, like God doesn't already know what's going on in our lives. Like he needs us to fill him in on what needs doing, as if we're giving him some divine honey-do list. The purpose of prayer is not to inform God what needs to be done on earth; the purpose of prayer is to align ourselves with his realities in heaven. Prayer is not him coming down—he's already here with us through his Spirit. Prayer is about us being lifted up; it's choosing to look up and beyond, choosing to yield to his ways and not begging like a spoiled child for our own desires to be fulfilled.

This kind of prayer, this kind of refocusing our attention on eternal things, requires practice and patience. When we become too earthly minded, we usually end up dissatisfied and desperate, aware of the frustration that Solomon expressed about the limitations of life as we know it. We must learn to focus on heaven and pray, "Your kingdom come, your will be done, on earth as it is in heaven," just as Jesus instructed us in the Lord's Prayer.

Maybe I'm old-fashioned, but I think our grandparents understood this principle. They didn't expect to have everything they wanted like we often do today. They seemed to display contentment and gratitude that transcended their circumstances and life's losses. So many of the old songs they loved were about heaven. "When we all get to heaven, what a day of rejoicing that will be!" Or, "Some glad morning when this life is o'er, I'll fly away." Singing these hymns helped them refocus regularly on the reality of eternity.

My grandfather often talked about heaven and how he longed to be reunited with our relatives "already invested on the other side." He envisioned something that filled him with a peace and a joy that didn't rely on what kind of car he drove, where he lived, or even the condition of his health. He knew there was more to this life than material comforts and sensual experiences.

PRAYER FORCE ONE

Another way to get a heavenly focus in our lives is to mix prayer with worship. Both prayer and worship change our view of reality by expanding our awareness of God's presence and reminding us to look beyond what we can see with our eyes. When we worship, we often begin with our world feeling so big and all-consuming, and God seeming so small and in the distance of our lives. Yet after we've worshiped, our perspective has righted itself, and we realize just how big he is and how small we are. When we practice fasting, we experience the ultimate separation from the world and focus singularly on him.

Adjusting our focus is often hardest when we're faced with an unexpected crisis or sudden loss. When my dad first told me he had cancer, I was crushed by the thought of losing him. I had always relied on his support and wisdom. I couldn't imagine life without him. As I began to absorb the shock, I wanted to surrender my fears and feelings before God. So I went into my office, closed the door, listened to worship music, and prayed. Later, when I emerged, I still felt devastated but also aware of the hope that comes from having an eternal perspective. By shifting my focus, I knew that God was still with me in the midst of this dark valley.

Please understand that I'm not encouraging you to focus on some kind of emotional placebo that makes you forget about your worries. God definitely cares about your concerns. But I've found that he often has an easier time revealing his solutions when you and I are concentrating on his ways instead of our own. From my own experiences, I've learned that God tends to be very practical in helping us find solutions bigger than our own perspective permits.

Several years ago I was reading the Birmingham newspaper and saw that our city was one of the top ten most violent cities in America.

Right there, in my own backyard, I discovered we were experiencing some of the worst crimes imaginable. I knew our church had to get involved, but I wasn't sure how. Because we believe the root of such problems is spiritual, I immediately went to our church's prayer coordinator and told him we had to do something about this.

As a result of our prayers and conversations, our church developed a strategy to systematically walk around our city in the highest crime areas and pray. Leading the procession was a pickup truck with speakers in the back sounding worship music. On our prayer walks, we asked for God's presence, protection, and provision. We immersed the city in our prayers that God's kingdom would reign where hell seemed to be bursting to life. We wanted our earth to be invaded by heaven.

Our chief of police, himself a former pastor, found out about our prayer walks and supported us by giving us police escorts while we walked and prayed. Other churches joined us each third Saturday of the month. The experience was unbelievable! Hundreds gathered each month for an hour-long prayer walk. Many people from our church also began to serve their community through projects like mentoring schoolkids and refurbishing homes.

For the past three years, our city has seen a double-digit decline in almost every category of crime. Credit also goes to our city leaders and the police force for their hard work and vision. But God has answered our prayers and changed our city!

SERVICE WITH A SMILE

Focusing on others and their needs also helps restore our perspective. When we're serving others, we're no longer obsessing about our own problems and the painful realities that may accompany them. Serving is one of the most eternal things we can do, one of the things that matters most. When we're addressing the needs of others and making their needs a priority over our own, we realize that our problems aren't as big as they sometimes seem. Jesus said, "Do not work for food that spoils, but for food that endures to eternal life" (John 6:27).

At our church, the individuals on our Dream Team use their gifts to serve others in our church and the community beyond. Whether it's painting rooms at the children's hospital, providing childcare for single moms, or leading a Bible study at a nursing home, they look for ways to help people experience the love of God.

I once talked with a guy who serves at one of the state prisons where our Sunday services are broadcast every week. He told me he'd been in church his whole life, but it was just not that important to him. He came to Highlands and rededicated his life to Christ, and started serving on the Dream Team. With tears in his eyes, he said that his faith had become so real because he now knew he was being used by God to reach the inmates in prison. Serving them gave him something to focus on, pray for, and live for.

I've found that the best way to pastor people is not always to focus on their individual needs but to focus them on the needs of others. There's nothing more satisfying than knowing we've made a positive difference, an eternal difference, in the lives of other people.

If we want to experience a breath of fresh air, we need to be in an empowering environment. When we discover the gifts God has placed inside us and exercise them by serving others, it's almost like we give ourselves the hit of pure oxygen that a winded athlete receives on the sidelines of a big game.

Another way to focus on serving others is to practice generosity.

By being a giver and not always a taker, we use our resources for eternal purposes. Giving is one of the most eternally significant ways we can serve. We're called to be stewards, not hoarders, of what God has given us. We can't take it with us, so we'd better send it on ahead, like those described in this verse: "They share freely and give generously to those in need. Their good deeds will be remembered forever. They will have influence and honor" (Psalm 112:9 NLT).

Keep in mind, I'm not talking about tithing here—the tithe is the Lord's, up front and off the top. We're not giving when we tithe; that is just a test to see if we will return what already belongs to God. No, I'm talking about living a generous life—giving our time, talents, and treasure away for no other reason than to bless others with God's love in hopes of making an eternal difference.

Every year our church gives out little "business cards" to our congregation that read, "A little something extra to show you God loves you." We tell people to take handfuls of them and show the love of God in practical ways—such as by paying for the order of the people in the car behind them in the fast-food drive-thru, then asking the clerk to give those people the card and tell them that the car ahead of them already paid for their meal. Some of our people leave a card with an especially generous cash tip for a server or barista. Others buy something they know someone else needs, such as back-to-school supplies, and leave them anonymously with the little card, explaining that the items are a gift.

Every year, we receive hundreds of calls, emails, and letters from people whose lives were blessed. We got a call from a lady who was given one of the cards at a fast-food drive-thru. She told us that she'd had every intention of taking her own life once she got home that day. She had stopped to get her "final meal" before she went home to commit suicide, but then someone ahead of her paid for her meal and left her the card. Surely that woman's life was worth so much more than the six bucks someone paid for her dinner! And I'm sure once the person who had bought her lunch heard the story, their problems suddenly seemed a whole lot smaller.

We gain a new perspective on our own problems when we focus on the needs of others.

TRAVELING LIGHT

Finally, the most significant thing we can do, the thing with the most eternal impact, is to share the good news of Jesus with someone. We can be a part of altering another person's eternal destiny. Knowing that heaven and hell are real, and knowing the scope of God's love and forgiveness, we should be sharing this ultimate breath of fresh air every opportunity we get. We should do it naturally and honestly, not in a way that feels contrived or pushy or artificial. But we should share our faith with a sense of urgency.

Remember Tanya, the woman sitting next to me on my flight who didn't like Christians? I described for you my conversation with her about how Christianity often has a branding problem, focusing more on religion rather than on relationship with God. Now let me share the rest of her story.

After I told Tanya that I shared her dislike for Christians hung up on religion, denominations, rule-keeping, and performance, I couldn't resist trying to change her perspective on what it means to really know Jesus. I challenged her not to let past experiences define her faith journey. I mentioned to her that our church had online services and encouraged her to watch the live service that week because I'd give her a shout-out.

Before I delivered the message that Sunday, I welcomed the online audience and gave Tanya a personal greeting. The following week she sent me an email addressed to "Pastor/Passenger Chris" in which she thanked me for the shout-out as well as for taking time during the flight to explain to her how she could make her relationship with God personal. "So simple," she said, "yet no one has ever explained it that way." Learning of her new openness and desire to grow closer to God made my day.

I share Tanya's response simply to show you what sharing our faith can look like in everyday life. I didn't hand her a tract or ask her to repeat a prayer after me. All I did was have a conversation with her. I was just being myself. In some ways, it would have been easier to remain quiet and anonymous, another passenger on a crowded flight. I could have focused on my own comfort and tried to take a nap. I could have worried about the problems that were waiting for me at home and at church. But I want to make as much of an eternal difference as possible. So when I can strike up a conversation with someone, I don't shy away from talking about my faith. If they find out I'm a pastor, and that leads us into discussing spiritual things, so be it.

BREATHING LESSON

One of the best ways for us to begin breathing fresh air again is by refocusing our lives on all that really matters—the eternal things. When we live for eternity, our difficulties don't disappear—but they don't weigh us down either. We can choose to focus on our problems even as we try to reach some imaginary place of trouble-free living. Or we can focus on eternal things and enjoy the fresh breeze of joyful purpose.

Live for eternity, and you'll never live another day unfulfilled.

God calls us to travel light by keeping our destination in sight. Spend some time today asking yourself, What am I currently doing that will have an eternal impact? What do I need to spend less time doing in order to focus more on the eternally significant goals to which God calls me?

Your responses to these questions will make a huge difference for all of eternity—one way or another. Don't miss out on the purpose for which God created you. Keeping your eyes on eternity will change the way you see everything.

> Let us throw off everything that hinders and the sin that so easily entangles. And let us run with perseverance the race marked out for us, fixing our eyes on Jesus, the pioneer and perfecter of faith.
>
> —Hebrews 12:1–2

5

ATTITUDE ADJUSTMENT

Attitude is a little thing that makes a big difference.

WINSTON CHURCHILL

The most life-giving, breath-filled person I've ever known was my father-in-law, Billy Hornsby.

Billy gave his heart to the Lord in 1972 after a coworker encouraged him to read the Bible. Raised as a Catholic, Billy had never really read the Scriptures before. But when he did, the Bible came alive and he gave his heart to Jesus.

Three years later, Billy and his family moved to West Monroe, a small town in northern Louisiana where he was stationed with the Louisiana State Police. His CB radio handle was "Reverend Smokey." Billy was so on fire for the Lord that when he pulled truckers over for speeding, he would also share the gospel with them. He always kept copies of the book of John in his police car to hand out to speeders. He called them his "captive audience."

Billy had a huge burden for Europe, and in 1984 he moved his whole family to Germany to plant and support churches all across the continent. That's where I met him. I was a youth pastor in Baton Rouge, and when I brought teams of students to Germany for summer missions, Billy and his family would host us. That's when I fell in love with Billy. You were probably thinking I was going to say that's when I fell in love with his daughter Tammy, but the truth is, I never even thought about Tammy until one day when the Hornsby family was back home in the United States for a short break.

Billy had taken me out to eat at Phil's Oyster Bar on Government Street in Baton Rouge. He asked me what I thought about his oldest daughter, Tammy, and he encouraged me to take her out on a date so I could get to know her. I always say that was the day Billy proposed to me. He always jokingly said that "many were called, but few were chosen," taking a quote from Jesus to express his love for me. So Tammy and I started dating, and at the end of every date, when I took Tammy home, she would go to bed while Billy and I stayed up for hours playing pool, talking, and dreaming big dreams for ministry.

To be honest, I still wasn't that interested in Tammy because she was so shy and called me "sir," since I was a pastor on staff. After a few months, Billy and the family went back to Germany, and just before they left, he told me that if I decided I couldn't live without Tammy, I should give him a call.

After months of letters and phone calls to her in Germany, I realized that I couldn't live without her. Tammy is the sweetest person I've ever met. I like to say she could teach the sun to be more consistent, because her loyalty, concern, and good nature never fluctuate. I actually flew to Germany with a ring and proposed to

Tammy there. Thank goodness she said yes. That's a long way to go to hear a no!

LIVE LIKE YOU'RE DYING

In 2009, Billy discovered a small sore on the bottom of his foot. At first doctors told him it wasn't anything to be concerned about. But when it wouldn't heal, the doctor decided to do a biopsy and found a stage 5 melanoma tumor on the bottom of his foot. The prognosis wasn't good, but Billy wasn't worried. He knew God could heal him—and if God didn't, he said, "I've already lived an incredibly full life—better than I ever hoped or dreamed."

In all his struggles through life, Billy never complained. In fact, in the twenty-seven years I knew Billy, I never saw him have a bad day. I never noticed him complaining about anything. And I never heard him say anything negative about anyone—ever.

On December 26, 2010, Billy preached what would be his final sermon at the church I pastor. He called his message "Struggle Well." He was honest about the fear, pain, fatigue, dread, and even doubt that accompany suffering. At the same time, he pointed us to the Word of God, saying, "The Word is your cure." He said that when we submit ourselves to God, who promises to never leave or forsake us, we can let go of fear and dread. "There's no fear in death," he said, "because the gospel is real."

"The more you dread tomorrow," he said, "the more you lose today. So when you wake up in the morning and start thinking about tomorrow, tell yourself, *I'm not going to do it. I'm going to make today a great day.*" As he was staring death in the face, Billy modeled courage, a positive attitude, and a deep faith. Even his doctors and nurses were blown away by his faith and peace.

The final three months of his life on earth were memorable, to say the least. Billy said they were the best weeks of his life. In January 2011, Billy had a near-death experience. We rushed him to the hospital and found out he had blood clots in his lungs. That night, he saw what he described as a set of stairs like those at a football stadium with a bright light at the end. He later said the Lord was giving him the opportunity to come to heaven right then if he wanted to. But Billy asked the Lord for a few more weeks so he could tell the people he cared for most how much he loved them and what they meant to him—and after about twenty-four hours, the light faded, the stairs disappeared, and he got better.

During the last eight weeks of Billy's life, he had over three hundred people, mostly out-of-town guests, visit him either in the hospital or at his house. Most came to pray for Billy and encourage him, but inevitably Billy would pray for and minister to them. I was there for most of these visits, and almost everyone who came hugged him and cried. Most of them said the same thing: "Thank you for believing in me."

One such visitor was a pastor whom my father-in-law had helped after this man's first two attempts at church planting had failed. Everyone, including the denomination this pastor was a part of, had given up on him. Not Billy. Billy encouraged him and connected him with ARC (Association of Relief Churches), our church-planting organization. This man's church now has thousands of members.

Billy finally went to be with Jesus on March 23, 2011. At the end of the day, he will not be known for what he did but for who he was. Billy loved God, and he loved people. He'd also made a choice to love life—food, fishing, hunting, music, and family—and he always made things fun. With Billy, every day was a great day.

LIFE OVERFLOWING

My father-in-law gave us a glimpse into what Jesus is like. It's clear that everyone—children, sinners, skeptics, the rich, the poor—loved being around Jesus. In fact, the only people who did not enjoy Jesus were the fake, inauthentic, self-righteous religious people. Everyone else was drawn to Jesus because he was enjoyable to be around.

One reason people loved being around Jesus was that he gave the people around him breath, life, energy, peace, and joy. He came to restore our relationship with God and to put fresh air back in our lives. Some people don't believe this and define their faith—or more accurately, their religion—as a series of do's and don'ts. I believe Jesus had people living in such joy-draining environments in mind when he said, "The thief comes only in order to steal and kill and destroy. I came that they may have and enjoy life, and have it in abundance (to the full, till it overflows)" (John 10:10 AMP).

People who have God's breath inside them seem to savor each day as a gift. Like my dear friend Billy, they enjoy life to the fullest. These people are winsome and attractive, which only draws others to them. They seem to relish each new day as one of promise and hope, opportunity and optimism. Their lives aren't any easier than anyone else's, and yet they rarely complain or dwell on their losses. They remember the past without remaining tied to it. They enjoy the present as a tremendous gift. They anticipate the future with great hope. They have influence and use it to positively encourage and shape those around them.

And yet from my experience, this is not how most of us live. Instead, we're pulled and pushed from one set of demands and expectations to another, from home to work to school to church, always reacting and trying to survive. There never seems to be time to be proactive and get ahead. But when we just go through the motions and try to keep up with everyone else, we lose our joy. We end up back in the doldrums, going around in circles, eventually wondering why we're doing what we're doing.

Real life comes from God living inside us, and we're more likely to experience a breath of fresh air when our attitudes reflect the light of his presence. And attitudes can be adjusted. Most of us develop an outlook over time that becomes our default way of seeing things. Our thoughts shape our emotions, which affect our perceptions, which influence our actions. If we want to get the wind back in our sails, we must begin by examining the fundamental thoughts we carry around inside us.

I'm convinced there are some foundational beliefs that we can harness and use as a wind generator in our lives. Let's look at some of them now.

FIRST, APPRECIATE LIFE

If joy is supposed to be a sign of our Christian faith, I'm afraid many of us are missing the mark. Most nonbelievers who watch us from a distance seem to view us the same way the movies portray Jesus—long-faced, serious, pious, gloomy, out of touch. But when we look at Scripture and consider the interactions Jesus had with those around him, we see that joy should indeed characterize our faith.

Satan has the world fooled into thinking that sin is exciting and fun and that serving God is boring and tedious. Of course, it's just the opposite. Ask anybody who's ever experienced the throes of an addiction and they'll tell you that nothing is more deadening and draining than doing the same thing over and over again with no true benefits. Because of the law of diminishing returns, our sinful attempts at pleasure provide less and less satisfaction. We realize how empty we feel and how disappointed we are.

So let's set the record straight. When we have a relationship with God as our Father and completely rely on him, our lives will never be boring again.

Just before going to the cross, Jesus explained to his disciples that they could experience the power and enjoy the love that existed between him and his heavenly Father. Then he said, "I have told you this so that my joy may be in you and that your joy may be complete" (John 15:11). Following the example of Jesus puts us on a grand adventure, one that will surprise and delight us much more than anything we could have ever dreamed up on our own.

We can't enjoy each day if we don't have a high appreciation for life. In order to cherish the life we've been given, we must never forget that God is working out his purposes for good. Even when we can't imagine it, even when times are hard and the pain feels unbearable, we must remember to exercise our faith and hope for God's best.

Paul reflects this kind of attitude when he describes his outlook in the midst of multiple hardships as "sorrowful, yet always rejoicing; poor, yet making many rich; having nothing, and yet possessing everything" (2 Corinthians 6:10). No matter what happened, Paul didn't let circumstances upset his peace or shake his faith. This is the attitude all of us can share when we place our trust in God. Though we may not yet understand how our situation will work out, we remain confident, knowing that God is taking care of it.

If you want to breathe new life into your attitude, you must be able to laugh. If you can't tell already—and I sure hope you can—I love to laugh. "There is a time for everything, and a season for every activity under the heavens"—and this includes "a time to laugh" (Ecclesiastes 3:1–4). Some people think it's inappropriate to laugh in church or irreverent to relate laughter with the sacredness of our faith in God. For them, church and religion are a serious business that requires the sobriety of a judge in a courtroom. But I believe that God loves laughter, which reflects a sense of joy in our lives. We're told, "A cheerful heart is good medicine" (Proverbs 17:22), and "The joy of the LORD is your strength" (Nehemiah 8:10).

Jesus certainly displayed joy and humor. Consider how people were drawn to him. Parents even brought their children to be blessed by him. Unlike his disciples, who scolded the adults for bothering their teacher, Jesus welcomed the children. Imagine someone who likes to have kids around. People like that typically have a twinkle in their eye and candy in their pockets.

The best day of your life is today, this one you're currently in. Accept the present as the gift God intends it to be and make the most of it. Don't squander it by worrying about the past or the future. Wake up and be in your life right at this moment.

PEOPLE WHO NEED PEOPLE

One of the best ways we experience our lives to the fullest is by loving people. Not just some people—everyone we encounter, even the ones we don't like.

Billy, my father-in-law, invited people into his world. He would take them out to eat, out hunting, out fishing, and even out on work projects. The closer he got to them and the closer he allowed them to get to him, the more they trusted, admired, and received from him. One of the life lessons I learned from watching Billy interact with others is that people can either irritate you or entertain you. They can either be considered a problem to be avoided or a person like you who just wants to be loved. As John Maxwell often says, people don't care how much you know until they know how much you care. Billy got that.

Many people point to other people as the reason they don't enjoy their lives. They've been wounded and disappointed so many times that they're skeptical, even cynical, about the motives of everyone they meet. They assume others are insincere and dishonest, unreliable and manipulative, just waiting to use or abuse them. So they stay defensive and on guard, either scaring people away with their harsh, unloving attitude, or else running away themselves. If this is the place where you find yourself, it's time to be healed of your bitterness. Consider what the Bible says: "The one who wants to enjoy life and see good days [good—whether apparent or not], must keep his tongue free from evil and his lips from speaking guile (treachery, deceit)" (1 Peter 3:10 AMP).

Our hearts become polluted with unresolved issues and old grudges when we allow someone else to get under our skin. Obviously, we didn't choose to be hurt, betrayed, or offended—but we always have a choice about how we react. And God makes it crystal clear how we must respond if we want to enjoy life. It's summed up by the word *forgiveness*.

If we don't forgive others, we're only hurting ourselves, not them. As the old adage reminds us, "Unforgiveness is like drinking poison and expecting someone else to die." Our unwillingness to forgive other people will keep us from experiencing and receiving the forgiveness our Father extends to us. If we're so obsessed with exacting revenge or getting an apology from someone who's hurt us, we're missing the point of God's grace.

One of the many things I appreciate about Jesus is how he loved the unlovely. Here he was, pure holiness and perfection, God come to earth, and yet he wasn't afraid to embrace imperfect, flawed, impure people. His holiness didn't drive people away—just the opposite! They were attracted to the life, the hope, the breath of fresh air that he offered them. Jesus had dinner with tax collectors. He freed a woman who had been caught in adultery and was about to be stoned. He healed those who were weak and in need.

Based on Jesus's example, we must make a decision about how we're going to treat other people. He accepted them, loved them, believed in them. He never piled guilt on them or condemned them as the religious leaders seemed to enjoy doing. He always respected people, encouraged them, offered them hope where they had given up. We're called to extend the same kind of love to those around us. That includes the incompetent boss or passive-aggressive supervisor, the grumpy teacher, and the inconsiderate neighbor, as well as the mean-spirited bully and the uptight attorney. Scripture makes it clear that we're called to put our faith into action: "Little children, let us stop just *saying* we love people; let us *really* love them, and *show it* by our *actions*" (1 John 3:18 TLB).

Of course, your love for others will find fuel in your love for God himself. As I shared earlier, my life message is to encourage people to draw closer to Jesus. That's because I know what it's like to move from a life-draining, exhausting, self-propelled faith to one that's life-giving, invigorating, and Spirit-propelled. Discover more of who God is. Enjoy the fullness of who he is as your Lord, your Father, your Creator. Look to him as your source of significance and satisfaction. How can you fall more deeply in love with your Savior? That is what the rest of this book is all about.

BAD ATTITUDE

Knowing how to adjust our attitudes can be easy; putting new practices in place can be another story. But we certainly didn't get the mindset we presently have overnight. It developed over time and through many different experiences. Similarly, it takes time and an ongoing commitment to practice the habits that can transform our attitudes.

First, I believe we must make a conscious choice every day about how we want to respond to what happens that day. It's so easy to blame other people, to hold on to grudges from the past, to keep our emotions knotted around devastating pain from injurious events. But we have a choice about how we're going to live.

We may not have had the same choices in the past, especially when we were growing up, but as adults we can choose how we will approach any challenges that come up. We can't determine what happens to us, but we can determine what happens *in* us. Paul makes the distinction very clear for us: "Let us throw off everything that hinders and the sin that so easily entangles. And let us run with perseverance the race marked out for us" (Hebrews 12:1).

I've found the best way to start off each day is by getting my mindset right. Maybe you're familiar with one of my favorite prayers:

Dear Lord,

So far today, I'm doing all right. I haven't gossiped, lost my temper, been greedy, grumpy, nasty, selfish, or self-indulgent. I have not whined, cursed, or eaten too much chocolate. However, I'm going to get out of bed in a few minutes, and I will need a lot more help after that. Amen.

Now that's funny! But seriously, when we begin each day by communicating with our Father, we're going to feel a whole lot more connected to him. If we take the time to let him know how much we love him and to ask him for help, we're making a choice about how our day will go.

Here's an even better prayer to pray: "May these words of my mouth and this meditation of my heart be pleasing in your sight, LORD, my Rock and my Redeemer" (Psalm 19:14).

When we begin the day by giving God thanks and worshiping him, we've grounded ourselves in what is real, in what matters most. No matter what happens that day, we know that God is in charge and working out his sovereign plan for good. When we acknowledge and appreciate what we have, we're not as inclined to look for green grass over the fence. We know that God provides for us and wants to bless us with his abundant generosity.

Another of the most refreshing choices we can make each day is to forgive—which, as we mentioned earlier, is also an attitude. Jesus not only told us to forgive others, but to do it quickly and to practice it as many times as necessary. That's why he told Peter we should forgive "seventy times seven" times when his disciple asked how many times we should forgive someone. Jesus didn't want us to forgive others just to let them off the hook; he knew doing so would put wind back in our sails.

One of the great scientists of our country, George Washington Carver, stated, "I will never let another man ruin my life by making me hate him." As an African American pioneering his scientific discoveries in a racially prejudiced society, I'm sure Carver had due cause to hate people who treated him unfairly. But he knew that the only way to move forward was to forgive. He knew he had a choice, and he decided he would never let someone else take that away from him, no matter what the offense.

Another hero of the faith to me was Billy's mom, a Cajun French woman named Williamette Plauche Hornsby. She was one of the sweetest souls you could ever hope to meet. Always in a good mood, always happy to see you, she was married to one of the hardest men you'd ever meet, my wife's grandfather. But his stubborn ways and hard-hearted decisions never seemed to affect Ma Maw Hornsby.

Anytime someone complained around her, she'd say, "Oh, pfff! Just forget about it. You've got the world by the tail." And she meant it. She had learned the art of letting go of the daily barbs and thorns that might come her way. There are many times now when I've been in a situation where I'm getting angry and, suddenly, I think of Ma Maw Hornsby. Thinking of her makes me smile because she was right—a forgiving attitude is liberating.

THIS IS GOOD

Maybe these principles and applications sound obvious or trite to you. But I assure you that if you truly want to live life to the fullest, to have real joy and peace and purpose and satisfaction, you have to avoid dismissing them as clichés or things you've heard before. You have to find a way to make these truths your own, to have them sink into your bones and become a part of who you really are. If you're still not sure how to do this, keep reading.

When you do begin to adjust your attitude and experience fresh wind in your sails, you'll discover a renewed appreciation for life. You won't take the hard times so seriously or so personally. You'll realize that each day is all you have. You'll love others and let them know it. You'll laugh at yourself and at the strange, wonderful, crazy things that happen in your life.

And sometimes, usually in hindsight, you'll see God's hand in places where you couldn't before—protecting you, guarding you, guiding you in ways that seemed hard at the time.

In 1999, when I was stuck in the doldrums, I sought God because I was desperate to get rid of my depression. Yet all the while, God was preparing to move me to Birmingham to plant a church. I just couldn't see it then.

People who have a high appreciation of life know that God is going to work everything out for the good. They may not always see it in this life, but they know they serve a good God who loves his children. They don't sweat the small stuff. They let their Father take care of it all. "And we know that in all things God works for the good of those who love him, who have been called according to his purpose" (Romans 8:28).

ARE YOU POSITIVE?

One of the simplest ways to adjust your attitude is to look for something positive in every situation. I'm not talking about becoming a Pollyanna who spiritualizes everything and pulls silver linings out of every storm cloud. I'm talking about being willing to see what you have in the midst of the storm.

Think about the people you know who complain about everything. They say things like, "This is it—I will never trust another living person again." My response to them: Really? Then you're in for a sad, sad life.

Or, "This is the worst thing that's ever happened to me—I'll never get over this." Are you sure? Most people experience pain in this life and manage to push through and keep going.

Or, "I really blew it this time!" Guess what? You'll probably blow it again. It's part of being human. But because you're human, you're able to fall down and get back on your feet again.

God designed us to be amazingly resilient. Whether it's rainy or sunny, stormy or calm, resilient people see the upside to their present position. They never lose sight of all they have to be grateful for because they've learned what Paul himself learned and passed on: "Give thanks in all circumstances; for this is God's will for you in Christ Jesus" (1 Thessalonians 5:18).

One of the most grateful people I've ever known was my grandmother, my dad's mom. We called her Ma Maw Hodges, and she lived to be ninety-four years old. She lived a hard life, but you would never have known it, judging by her attitude. She was orphaned at age thirteen when her mother burned to death while boiling their clothes to avoid diphtheria. Ma Maw Hodges grew up and married the man who was my dad's father. Then the unbelievable happened. Her husband was killed in a car wreck, leaving her with a one-year-old son (my dad) to raise.

Undaunted, she worked two jobs and brought up her son to be positive and hardworking, not a bitter victim of circumstance. Eventually, she married again, and her son took his stepfather's name. (So I'm not really a Hodges by blood; my biological grandfather's name was Hampton.) As she grew older, my grandmother suffered from crippling arthritis for many years. But I never heard her complain—not once.

Whenever anyone asked her how she was doing, Ma Maw Hodges's answer was always the same: "I'm better off than most." Her attitude was inspiring—like a breath of fresh air. Many times throughout her life, she chose to be happy. She knew the meaning of one of her favorite verses:

> Whatever is true, whatever is noble, whatever is right, whatever is pure, whatever is lovely, whatever is admirable—if anything is excellent or praiseworthy—think about such things. (Philippians 4:8)

A NEW ATTITUDE

Finally, if we want to experience fresh air in our attitudes, we must turn all our worries over to God. One of the primary reasons we're not happy is that we try to handle everything ourselves. Yet no one can handle everything—or even most things—in their lives. No matter how much money we have, no matter how advanced our technology becomes, humans will always be limited. In many ways, we basically make the same mistake Adam and Eve made in the garden, which is choosing to think we can be like God, over and over again.

The difficulties we face can't be our problem and God's problem at the same time. When we realize that he's in control, that he alone is God and is infinite, powerful, loving, and all-knowing, it's suddenly much easier to relax and enjoy the present moment. He never intended for us to worry about what might happen, what could happen, what should happen, or what will happen. He only asks that we follow him and live in this moment right now. We're told:

> Do not be anxious about anything, but in every situation, by prayer and petition, with thanksgiving, present your requests to God. And the peace of God, which transcends all understanding, will guard your hearts and your minds in Christ Jesus. (Philippians 4:6–7)

Notice that prayer and thanksgiving are gifts God offers us so that we may access his peace. We can also rest and be refreshed in his presence as we read Scripture, pray, worship, and serve others—some of the practices we'll look at in the coming chapters.

God wants us to rely on him. "Cast all your anxiety on him because he cares for you" (1 Peter 5:7). When we give him our concerns, we naturally have an attitude that's worry-free, that's at peace, that's present to love those around us.

Like my father-in-law or the wonderful grandmothers in our family, we can be a force for good in this life. We can display the heart of Christ in everything we do, showing others who God really is. We can be content and compassionate, relaxed and resilient.

BREATHING LESSON

One of the healthiest things you can do is take responsibility for your own attitude. The key is to focus on what happens *in* you, not *to* you. Attitude is a choice. And for most of us, our attitude will not take care of itself. We need to manage it every day.

The choice is ours. On the day Billy died, I promised the Lord that I would do everything I could to live my life the way Billy did.

By spending time watching people like Billy, Ma Maw Hornsby, and Ma Maw Hodges who attracted other people to them by their joy, good humor, and love, I learned to begin adopting a similar outlook. Who has modeled the character of Jesus for you in your life? How have they influenced you to grow closer to God and be a life-giver? I encourage you to let their example be an inspiration and a model for you to follow, so that you as well become a breath of fresh air to others.

> Let the Spirit renew your thoughts and attitudes. . . . Imitate God, therefore, in everything you do, because you are his dear children. Live a life filled with love, following the example of Christ.
>
> —Ephesians 4:23; 5:1–2 NLT

6

THE BOOK IS ALIVE

To what greater inspiration and counsel can we turn than to the imperishable truth to be found in this treasure house, the Bible?

QUEEN ELIZABETH II

When my wife and I first got married, we lived in a little eight-hundred-square-foot town house in Baton Rouge. It qualified as a town house simply because it had an upstairs with a tiny bedroom, but not much more. We didn't mind the close quarters, though. Like most newlyweds, we were happy just to be together.

One morning, after we'd been there for about a year, Tammy and I came downstairs and couldn't believe our eyes. The entire first floor of our little home had been stripped bare! You know how the homes in Whoville looked after the Grinch came and took everything? Well, he must have paid us a visit because it was cleaner than when we'd moved in. Both the front door and back door, only about thirty feet apart, were swinging wide open.

We ran outside to the little parking lot of our complex, and sure enough, both our cars parked in front had also been broken into. We were speechless. We just looked at each other with disbelief through tearful eyes. How had we been able to sleep through such a huge theft? Our stereo, TV, VCR, kitchen appliances, even our cars' cassette players had been stolen, never to be seen by us again.

If you've ever been violated by a crime like this, you know that you lose more than just your possessions. You lose your peace of mind. Your sense of security and your ability to relax go out the door with your property. You have trouble sleeping because the thieves know where you live and know how to get into your home. You're scared and paranoid about being robbed again. You can't help it. You try to be tough, but inside you're terrified of it happening again, and you feel powerless to do anything about it.

In the days that followed, my wife and I prayed, met with the police, talked with friends, family, and each other, and did everything we could to turn our loss over to God and move on with our lives. Nothing seemed to work until the day we found this passage in the Psalms: "There will be no breaching of walls, no going into captivity, no cry of distress in our streets. Blessed is the people of whom this is true; blessed is the people whose God is the Lord" (144:14–15).

The words felt tailor-made for us and our situation. God was still larger and more powerful than any thief, any robber, any thug who violated our home and stole our property. God would deal with them on his terms, so we didn't have to worry about it. And we didn't have to be afraid any longer; God would always be our protection and refuge.

Tammy and I printed that passage on a couple of index cards and stuck one on the front door and the other on the back door. We posted God's Word as a guard around our house. It wasn't like a magic barrier or anything like that, although—as we'll discuss in a moment—the Scriptures definitely contain God's power and authority. We posted those verses to remind us of what was true—that God was with us no matter what. Every time we saw one of those cards, our confidence grew and our fear subsided.

DAILY CHORES

As you think about my story, keep in mind what I've already told you about my early life as a Christian: I spent time in the doldrums. This included a flat prayer life and an indifference about the Word of God. I certainly respected the Bible as divine and inerrant, and I knew I was supposed to study it and learn about God and his character. I knew it was the ultimate handbook for how to live a purpose-driven, fulfilled life as a follower of Jesus. And yet, it seemed like pure drudgery to read my Bible on a daily basis, a chore that had to be done just so I could say I did it before getting on with my day.

It was like making the bed or doing the dishes. You couldn't just do it once and then let it go for months and months. If you were a good Christian, you did it every day, or at least several times a week. But that didn't mean it would be enjoyable or even relevant to what was going on in your life. It was just a good practice to remind yourself and others that you took your faith seriously.

Can you relate to my experience? How would you describe your relationship with your Bible right now? Do you feel a twinge of guilt when the topic comes up because you feel like you should read it more often? Or do you feel a sense of satisfaction because you read God's Word this morning?

Let me challenge you. Think not only about the last time you read your Bible but also about what you read. What stuck with you?

In those years past, not much had been sticking with me. But after the break-in, and in other times of need, I began to see the Bible differently. I had a new appreciation for how God's Word applied to my everyday life. And as my sails filled with the breath of God, and my passion and excitement for my faith expanded, I began to realize that I had to rethink my view of the Bible. I didn't want to take it for granted or approach reading it as a chore.

Imagine coming home to discover that your spouse has sent the kids to their grandparents and a special dinner for two awaits you. There's candlelight and soft music playing, and your spouse is all dressed up. Would you respond by saying, "Again? Do we have to have another romantic dinner and kiss and stuff? Okay, whatever . . ." That would be pretty insulting, wouldn't it? I wonder if God feels that way when we regard his Word so dispassionately.

The Bible is obviously indispensable to the Christian faith. If you attempt to follow Jesus without it, you're not going to get far. But the Bible is much more than an ancient manual full of historical stories and dos and don'ts. It's a divine wind machine, inflating our sails with God's breath, giving us direction and purpose, and propelling us forward. Jesus said, "The Spirit gives life; the flesh counts for nothing. The words I have spoken to you—they are full of the Spirit and life" (John 6:63; in the New Testament's original Greek, the word *spirit* literally means "breath").

Jesus is telling us that his words, the messages that he came to deliver, are not normal words. Basically he's saying, "These words

I've spoken to you are breath, a blast of wind to give you life." Or put another way, "My words are fresh air for you."

POWER WORDS

The entire Bible has this kind of strength, as I see it. God's Word has the power to bring about its own fulfillment. It's alive and dynamic and meets you where you are, if you let it sink into your heart and mind. Like a compass that's always at true north, it can dramatically alter your life's course and show you who God is and who you are. It can transform the way you live and help you discern what's from God and what's not. In fact, it tells us what it can do:

> The word of God is alive and active. Sharper than any double-edged sword, it penetrates even to dividing soul and spirit, joints and marrow; it judges the thoughts and attitudes of the heart. (Hebrews 4:12)

God's Word is alive, and if you'll let it, it will cut through anything you face. So don't just read the Bible; let the Bible read you. As you do, the Bible will align your emotions and mind with God as you make day-to-day decisions. There's nothing too difficult, too painful, too embarrassing, too human, or too earthy for it to address. The people populating its pages can inspire you, coach you, challenge you, instruct you, and sometimes amaze you, if you'll let them.

So how do you and I get there? How can we reach the point where reading the Bible engages us and brings us joy and helps us interact with God? Like dough that needs an ingredient to make it rise, the Bible requires our faith in order to be activated in our lives. Faith serves as the catalyst that enables us to take the necessary steps of obedience as we follow God and listen to his Word.

Why did the Israelites have to wander around the desert for forty years rather than march right into the land God had promised them? According to the New Testament, they heard God's words but didn't trust him to fulfill what he had promised: "We also have had the good news proclaimed to us, just as they did; but the message they heard was of no value to them, because they did not share the faith of those who obeyed" (Hebrews 4:2).

Reading the Word only out of a sense of duty is like trying to make dynamite without nitroglycerin. It simply won't ignite. When we don't have faith, or we don't bring it to our encounter with the Word, we view it in a flat, lifeless way that many would say feels "boring."

Has that been your experience? Maybe you've read the Bible and it was of no value because you just didn't get it. Or you went to church and listened to a message and it was like hearing someone lecture in a foreign language because it just didn't seem to make much sense. According to that verse from Hebrews, when you lack faith as you read God's Word, its truth can't take root in your heart and life.

Okay, Chris, you may be thinking, you're telling me that I don't have enough faith for the Bible to come alive. So what am I supposed to do about it? I'm not sure I can just flip a switch and make all this God stuff work.

I hear you. Maybe you're thinking, I've had times when the Scriptures seemed alive and relevant to me, but I seem to have lost it. How much faith do I need to get back to that place?

Another fair question.

In fact, if you think you have to conjure up faith on your own, you'll always be frustrated. The key ingredient in making faith work is God's revelation. Let me explain.

Have you ever tried to solve a problem for a while when suddenly the solution seemed crystal clear and you wanted to shout, "Eureka!"? God's revelation is the aha moment when you connect the dots and realize not only what the real problem is, but how it pertains to your life and what to do about it. Every time a passage from the Bible makes you think, *Now I understand; now the Bible has totally come alive to me*, your faith is activated.

Curiously enough, in Greek (the language used for the original manuscripts of the New Testament) there are two different terms for the word *word*. One is used to describe the kind of insight and illumination we've been talking about, an epiphany where all the lights come on. This word is *rhema*, and it is distinct from the Greek word for *word—logos*, which refers to the literal words on the page as you're reading them now. *Rhema* is more than just the words themselves; it's the process of understanding them, of having eyes to see and ears to hear. It's almost like reading between the lines so that you get a sense of the real message and its relevance and application to your life.

THE AHA MOMENT

So many of us get stuck focusing just on the *logos* (the written word) that we don't press into having a deeper encounter with the *rhema* (the revealed word). Remember that you're going to need faith if God's Word is going to come alive for you, and in order to have your faith activated, you need to experience revelation.

Let me give you one of the best examples of this kind of revelation I can think of. You've probably heard how the angel Gabriel visited a teenage girl named Mary to let her know she would become pregnant with a child who would be the Messiah her people longed for. Some scholars say that Mary was between thirteen and sixteen years old. If you have kids, especially teenagers, this fact may blow your mind. Here's this young lady, minding her own business, when an angel drops in to tell her, "God finds favor with you and has an assignment for you if you're willing to do it. You're going to be the mother of his baby, okay?"

Mary responds like most of us would in her situation: "How can this be? I'm still a virgin." At this point, the communication between the two of them is at the *logos* level. The angel is saying something that is entirely true, and yet Mary can't comprehend his message because it doesn't make sense logically. It defies what she knows about human reproduction.

Here's where the aha moment kicks in. The angel explains, "Here's how it's going to happen. The Holy Spirit, the wind and the breath of God, is going to enter you, and he is actually going to overshadow you so that this child will be conceived immaculately." Then the angel Gabriel adds the key phrase: "*Nothing* will be impossible with God" (Luke 1:37 ESV).

Now, this may sound like a great motivational bumper sticker to us, but it's so much more. In the Greek, the expression for "nothing" is actually two words: "no word [*rhema*]." So let me put it together for you with this in mind. Basically the angel tells Mary, "I know you may not get it now, but if what I'm saying ever becomes a revelation to you, then nothing is impossible." Or here's my translation: No word that God speaks, when it becomes a revelation to you, will lack the power for its fulfillment. There's nothing in the

Bible that lacks the power to actually happen inside you, when it becomes an "Oh, now I get it!" moment.

Mary gets it. She tells the angel, "I am the Lord's servant. May your word to me be fulfilled" (Luke 1:38). How does she get it? And better yet, how do we get it?

Let's clarify this process by thinking it through:

Faith activates the Word.

So how do you grow your faith?

Revelation activates faith.

And how do you get a revelation?

Meditation on Scripture activates a revelation.

Let's talk about this last one next.

CHEW YOUR FOOD

Throughout the Old and New Testaments, we're told numerous times in numerous ways to meditate on God's Word. The Old Testament was originally written in Hebrew, and one of the meanings for the Hebrew word for *meditate* is "rumination," the same word used to describe a cow chewing its cud. (In fact, the process of rechewing the cud to further break down plant matter and stimulate digestion is called *ruminating*.)

Now, if you don't have a farming background, you may wonder what it means for a cow to chew its cud—and what's a cud, anyway? As gross as it sounds, *cud* is the food a cow ingests, chews, swallows, regurgitates, then chews some more before swallowing again. According to animal scientists, cows spend about eight hours a day at this, which works out to about thirty thousand chews. For their digestive systems, it's critical that cows keep chewing over and over again to moisten their food and break it down into smaller pieces.[1]

Similarly, we should meditate on God's Word in such a way that it stays with us. We're so bombarded with information each day—emails, social media messages, reports, articles, letters, notes, magazines, and books. It's gotten to the point that most of us don't read anymore; we skim. We usually comprehend only what we need in the moment, then it's on to the next task. Rarely do we read something and ponder it, then go back to reread and ponder it again.

But we're told, "Keep this Book of the Law always on your lips; *meditate* on it"—chew, swallow, regurgitate, and chew it some more so you get all its flavor. And do this "day and night, so that you may be careful to do everything written in it. *Then* you will be prosperous and successful" (Joshua 1:8).

I want what's after *then* ("prosperous and successful") but need to do what's before *then* ("meditate"). If you and I want the Bible to be revealed, we need to commit to meditating on it.

THE LAST WORD

In order to experience the breath of life that comes from reading the Bible, and in order for Scripture to come alive and remain dynamic in all areas of our lives, we need to focus on three key principles.[2]

First, we must accept Scripture's authority. We live in a culture that seems to intentionally attack the authority and validity of God's Word. Rather than letting it change them, many people seem to want to change the Bible to fit their preferences. Hollywood and the news media often do this, and even the church has done it sometimes.

According to findings from the Cultural Research Center at Arizona Christian University, only about 4 percent of U.S. adults hold a biblical worldview, and Barna polls reflect similar numbers.[3]

Although I realize I may be outnumbered, I boldly proclaim that I'm in that 4 percent minority of people who believe that the Bible is alive, perfect, totally relevant, totally true, righteous, holy, and from God. The Word of God is timeless and transcends cultures and nationalities and denominations. It has the final say on all aspects of our lives. It truly has the last word.

When we accept the authority of the Bible, we commit to reading it and then taking what it says as the ultimate source of truth. That's the approach the apostle Paul commends:

> We never stop thanking God that when you received his message from us, you didn't think of our words as mere human ideas. You accepted what we said as the very word of God—which, of course, it is. And this word continues to work in you who believe. (1 Thessalonians 2:13 NLT)

The psalmist tells us that blessed are those who "delight in the law of the Lord, meditating on it day and night"; they don't "join in with mockers" who scorn God and his Word (Psalm 1:1–2 NLT). He goes on to say that people who respect God's Word are like trees firmly planted by a stream of water, whose leaves never wither. Whatever they set their hands to will prosper.

When you're in doubt or uncertain, when you're confused or frustrated, turn to Scripture. "All Scripture is God-breathed and is useful for teaching, rebuking, correcting and training in righteousness" (2 Timothy 3:16). When you give the Bible the authority it deserves, it will speak into your life with clarity and certainty.

You'll go from merely reading words on the page—*logos*—to having ongoing aha moments, or *rhema*.

DAILY DIET

Next, we must make our relationship with the Bible part of our everyday lives. We are to be in the Word every day, not out of duty or to feel better about ourselves, but because doing so gives us room to meditate, which is the pathway to revelation and faith. The Bible is not a once-a-week, only-on-Sunday kind of book. It's not even a morning devotional book. Instead it's like food, something you and I need every day. Something to be devoured and digested, chewed on and chewed some more.

Too often, we allow someone to serve us a tiny Bible morsel on a platter once a week, then we wonder why we're weak, stuck in one place, or lost in the doldrums. I don't know about you, but I don't eat three meals a day. I eat about five times a day. I get up in the morning and eat something. That usually holds me until lunch. When I get hungry again around three or four in the afternoon, I have a snack. Then there's dinner around six and usually another snack before bedtime. Yep, I pretty much eat all day long!

One of my favorite Bible reading practices is using the *One Year Bible*, which has daily passages from the Old Testament, New Testament, Psalms, and Proverbs. Each day's reading takes only about fifteen minutes. At year's end, I've read through the whole Bible. I try to find just one verse from all the readings for that day that I can chew on all day long, returning to get more bites throughout the day. I may even try to memorize a verse or print it on a little card to carry around with me.

Sometimes I meditate on a verse that comes from a concern that I need to turn over to the Lord. Earlier I mentioned how the passage from Psalm 144 comforted and restored Tammy and me after the burglary in our home. When our kids started driving, I paraphrased Psalm 121:8 and kept it in front of me: "The Lord will watch over your coming and going both now and forevermore." I'm not sure who needed the blessing more in this case—me for my nerves or my kids for their driving! Surely God knows how much better they drive than I do.

Are you often afraid and finding yourself lying awake at night worrying? Try Psalm 27:1—"The Lord is my light and my salvation—whom shall I fear?"

Do you have money issues going on? Then know and understand Philippians 4:19—"My God will meet all your needs according to the riches of his glory in Christ Jesus."

The third and final thing to remember is quite simple: *Just do it.* Accept the Bible's authority, make it an ongoing part of your everyday life, then put it into practice. Live it, do it, practice it. When God's Word says to love, put it into practice. When it says to give, give. "Don't just listen to God's word. You must do what it says. Otherwise, you are only fooling yourselves" (James 1:22 NLT).

Our goal should be to take the living Word and plant it into the world around us. Into our relationships and our work. Into our classrooms and our cubicles. Into our kitchens and our bedrooms. Into our bank accounts and our bill paying. *Everywhere.*

BREATHING LESSON

The Bible is not a normal book. Its words aren't just text on a page; they contain supernatural power to attain their own fulfillment. The Bible has breath in it, the God-essence that makes all the difference in the world. If you want to experience transformation—to live a vibrant adventure instead of spin circles in the doldrums—read your Bible and let it propel you forward.

The next step is up to you. Read the Bible daily, because it's alive and the only book that ultimately matters. Then *live* it.

> In the beginning was the Word, and the Word was with God, and the Word was God. He was with God in the beginning. Through him all things were made; without him nothing was made that has been made. In him was life, and that life was the light of all mankind. The light shines in the darkness, and the darkness has not overcome it.
>
> —John 1:1–5

7

ENJOYING PRAYER

To be a Christian without prayer is no more possible than to be alive without breathing.

MARTIN LUTHER KING JR.

As much as we might think otherwise, *enjoying prayer* is not an oxymoron, like jumbo shrimp or icy hot. From my experience, both personally and as a pastor, if there's one area where people find the least amount of enjoyment, it's with prayer. We all know we need to do it, but few Christians have been able to discover how to enjoy taking the time to talk to God.

If, like me, you were raised in the church, there's a good chance that prayer became something detached from the rest of your faith—something lifeless, boring, stagnant. It was a speech to be endured, like a teacher's lecture, or words that you knew were important but that seemed to run together, like the fire marshal's code. As I've studied prayer in the Bible, I've discovered that most people today pray very differently from what's described in Scripture. There's not one place where it says that when you pray you should close your eyes. And there's certainly not one place where it tells you to speak in a soft, quiet, reverent monotone, addressing God as if he were from England. (I think some people assume it must be more official if you pray like the King James Version—"Thou knowest of what I speaketh.") Imagine addressing your spouse and kids as if you'd just stepped out of one of Shakespeare's plays!

Also, prayer can feel like drudgery if you worry too much about how long you pray. I remember once as a teenager hearing a sermon on Jesus and his disciples in the garden of Gethsemane. The preacher told us that Jesus got after his disciples because they couldn't watch with him for an hour. Likewise, we were told, if we spent anything less than an hour in prayer, we weren't pleasing God either. I went home that day utterly discouraged. I had finally managed to pray fifteen minutes at a stretch, and now I had been told my prayer life was an utter failure.

Prayer is not nearly that complicated. Honestly, you are simply talking with someone you know and love. I'm a little embarrassed to share something so personal, but when I wake up in the morning, I tell God, "Good morning, Lord. It's good to see you. I've missed you. I'm glad we get to spend a few minutes together right now. I'm so grateful for how much you love me. You're my daddy, my Abba Father, and I love you today with all my heart."

If that sounds like something a child might pray, then I'm glad. That's how I want to approach God, as a son who's excited to love and serve his Father. When you pray, it really is just a conversation between you and the One who loves you most. Prayer can be one of the most dynamic, life-giving, breath-of-fresh-air places in your entire life.

Jesus certainly prayed a lot. In fact, all Jewish people learned how to pray when they were very young. They not only knew how to pray, but they had memorized prayers and knew when to use them and for which occasions. It was not only part of the religious practice but also a cultural custom. Keeping this in mind, it's all the more interesting to read that Jesus's disciples asked him to teach them to pray. "One day Jesus was praying in a certain place. When he finished, one of his disciples said to him, 'Lord, teach us to pray'" (Luke 11:1).

PRAYER 101

Now here's my theory about this rather unique request: Since these Jewish disciples already knew how to pray based on their cultural upbringing, I don't think they were asking Jesus to teach them *how* to pray. Instead, I believe they were saying, "We don't know how to pray like you do—to receive that life-giving, breath-of-fresh-air experience that comes not from just saying a memorized prayer, but from being in conversation with God. When we pray, it doesn't look like that, not at all. Can you teach us to pray with passion, like we mean it?"

Jesus's response, of course, is the best-known prayer in the world, the Lord's Prayer. He said to his disciples, "Okay, I can teach you. After this manner, pray this. . . ." I believe Jesus then did what rabbis have always done down through the ages when instructing their students in any area. He taught his followers the *topics* of prayer that they should bring before God. However, two thousand years later, we have turned the instructions into a prayer in and of itself. In my humble opinion, the Lord's Prayer was never intended by Jesus to be prayed verbatim just as he spoke it. It's okay if we do, but there's so much more to it than that.

When we recite the Lord's Prayer, or any prayer, from memory over and over again, there's always the danger that we're not considering exactly what we're saying. While I certainly seem to have topics and themes that come up a lot when I talk to my wife and kids ("Okay, there goes Dad again . . ."), I don't have a paragraph that I repeat word for word every time we talk.

I'm not criticizing anyone for praying the Lord's Prayer as it appears in Scripture. I'm only noting that the words themselves are not as important as the topics Jesus is covering in his model prayer. Basically, what he gives to his disciples, including us, is an outline for our communication with God:

> Our Father which art in heaven, Hallowed be thy name. Thy kingdom come, Thy will be done in earth, as it is in heaven. Give us this day our daily bread. And forgive us our debts, as we forgive our debtors. And lead us not into temptation, but deliver us from evil: For thine is the kingdom, and the power, and the glory, for ever. Amen. (Matthew 6:9–13 KJV)

Jesus's prayer outline has seven items based on the seven phrases that he uses. Let's look at them together and see how they can breathe fresh air into the way we talk to our Father.

TAKE IT PERSONALLY

Notice how Jesus begins his instruction on prayer. The first thing he teaches us to do is connect with God relationally—with *our*

Father who is in heaven. It's so important when we enter into our prayer time that we do as Jesus does and begin by calling God something that's endearing. So often we treat him like some distant, impersonal machine: "Oh, great and mighty God, we give Thee thanks . . ."

Jesus says, "You want to know my secret? Here's what you do. You begin with the assurance that God is your Father and loves you like a daddy loves his children. He wants to be in this relationship with you, not just as your God but as your Father."

Now, addressing God as our dad may be a hurdle for some of us who had less-than-honorable earthly fathers. Many of us struggle to relate to God so intimately, and the word *father* may even conjure up negative images because of the baggage we have with our own dads. We're more comfortable keeping God at arm's length.

So much about our relationship with God depends on how accurately we see him. If we view him as the loving daddy he is, with his arms open wide, waiting to hold us, we're going to enjoy spending time with him in conversation. However, if we view him as a faceless, angry giant with a club in his hand waiting to pounce on us, it's no wonder we try to avoid him.

I used to struggle with how I viewed God. My view of him was based on an evangelism tract that depicted God as a cartoon-like king sitting on a big throne, the kind of chair that the statue of Honest Abe sits in at the Lincoln Memorial. In the tract, God had no discernible features, just a glowing light all around him. The cartoon people, by comparison, looked like little ants beside his feet.

Another image I had of God came from one of my favorite movies growing up, *The Wizard of Oz*. God was just like the Mighty

Oz—a big, scowling, green face enveloped in smoke, with a booming voice that told us to go do spiritual things: PRAY! PERFORM FOR ME!

Obviously, there was nothing positive about my mental image of God. Even as I got older and knew that God wasn't like my imagined version of him, I still struggled to know how to relate to him. That began to change as I studied the Bible and saw how close Jesus was to his Dad. Jesus brought us the freedom to relate to God in this same way.

Paul wrote:

> Those who are led by the Spirit of God are the children of God. The Spirit you received does not make you slaves, so that you live in fear again; rather, the Spirit you received brought about your adoption to sonship. And by him we cry, "Abba, Father." (Romans 8:14–15)

The Greek word here for "Spirit" is *pneuma*, meaning "God's breath of fresh air." Consider my translation based on this notion: God wants to put breath back in our sails through the fresh air of his Spirit because he's adopted us as his children.

So now we don't have to tremble like the Cowardly Lion before the Mighty Oz. We can run to our heavenly Father the way our own children run to greet us when we come home. The Aramaic word Paul uses here, *Abba*, is sometimes rendered as "Daddy," but it's warmer than that, more familiar. It's like "Papa! I'm so glad to see you!" all rolled into one word. When I came to this realization about how we can relate to him, my old image of God went up in smoke. He is someone who wants to be with me and spend time with me.

THE NAMES OF GOD

Once we've established our relationship with God, Jesus tells us to honor our Father's name: "Hallowed be thy name." God's names—and he has many, each expressing a different facet of his magnificent being—have incredible power. According to Proverbs 18:10, his names are places of protection; the righteous can run there and be safe.

In this part of the Lord's Prayer, I picture Jesus telling us, "Look, the next thing to consider after you establish your personal relationship, your greeting, is the benefit you have in honoring God's names." We call him our Righteousness and remember that he has made us righteous. We're reminded that we don't have to depend on our own efforts anymore by making animal sacrifices and following the old letter of the Law.

As you may be aware, there are many names for God throughout the Scriptures. He is our Peace, our Protector, our Provider, and the list goes on. Each name carries with it a reminder of the distinct benefits we have in that aspect of God's relationship with us. We call out to him and we remember that he is a God who provides, a God who gives shelter, comfort, and the peace that passes understanding.

HIS AGENDA FIRST

Next, Jesus lets us in on the real secret to our relationship with God—the key to how we talk to him. "Thy kingdom come, Thy will be done in earth, as it is in heaven." In other words, we need to pray and seek God's agenda first. Isn't it true that so often when we pray, we've got our laundry list of things to ask him for? But Jesus reminds us to first focus on what he wants done. When we follow his way of doing things and allow him to guide us, he takes care of us by listening to our needs—our "daily bread."

Have you ever noticed how much easier it is to relate to someone when you're willing to participate in their agenda before asking something of them? I recall a time when we had some major yard work that needed to be done after a big storm, so I enlisted my sons to help. We were out lifting tree limbs, mowing and raking grass, and picking up rocks and sticks. My guys had the best attitude—they were doing a great job and doing it gladly. Well, all except my youngest, Joseph, who definitely didn't have yard work on his agenda for the day. At one point, he walked by me with a little stick and said, "You can thank me later."

When we finished several hours later, I wanted to do something special for my hardworking guys, so I grilled some burgers and we had a great dinner. As we were sitting around afterward, my middle son, David, said, "Hey, Dad—are you thinking it's a Krispy Kreme kind of night?" My immediate thought was, *Definitely! How many do you want?*—because I remembered what a great job my boys had done and how great their attitudes had been. Since they'd gladly participated in what I needed them to do, I was happy to do what they wanted in return.

It's so easy for us to become nearsighted and focus our prayers only on ourselves. "Thy kingdom come, Thy will be done" keeps us farsighted—attentive to God's agenda first. And if we want to know what our Father's primary agenda is, I don't think we have to look far.

Foremost, he clearly wants to rescue those who are estranged from him, the lost sheep who've wandered off, the prodigals and the prostitutes, the tax collectors and the weak. Again and again, he tells us to seek the lost, take care of those in need, and serve one another generously and graciously. We are God's conduits—his hands and feet and eyes and ears—here on earth. We're blessed when we give to others as he gives to us. Anytime we put our efforts and energies into reaching those in need, our Father is pleased and honored.

OUR NEEDS

Once we've addressed our Father, honored the fullness of who he is through his many names, and focused on his agenda, Jesus tells us that it's then time to ask God to meet our needs. "Give us this day our daily bread." Notice how comprehensive this request is. We're not merely asking God to be involved in our area of greatest need or sharpest struggle; we're asking him to provide his presence and provision for us in all areas of our lives. Put simply, we should depend on him for everything, regularly. Bread gets stale and spoils if it's not eaten. We need fresh bread on a daily basis.

We tend to focus on the problems, the needs, the deficits, and the trials. But we don't need God's help only when we give the big presentation at work; we also need him while we're driving to work, interacting with our assistant, meeting with our boss, talking on the phone, and returning email.

Jesus told us to pray in a way that acknowledges our Source. "God, everything I have comes from you. You're my source for all that I'm entrusted to steward. I wouldn't even get to work if you didn't give me breath to wake up this morning. You're my source for *everything*. So, Lord, give me today and everything I need throughout it."

I love how this verse from the Psalms expresses the same idea: "I look up to the mountains—does my help come from there? My help comes from the Lord, who made heaven and earth!" (121:1–2 NLT). Does our help come from our boss or the government or our accountant or our ability to work harder? No. It all comes from God, who made heaven and earth.

A MATTER OF THE HEART

Once we've acknowledged God as the source of all we already have, and once we've trusted him to provide all we need, Jesus leads us next into a critical part of the prayer, a touchy area: "and forgive us our debts, as we forgive our debtors." If we want our lives to be propelled by God's breath and to move forward effortlessly, our hearts must be right with God and with other people. One of the most liberating, energizing things we can do each day is go to our Father and ask his forgiveness.

In fact, I would encourage you to take it a step further and pray as David prayed (as in Psalm 139:23) for God to search you, know you, and test your sincerity. Ask him to point out any blind spots or areas that you may not realize need attention. If there's any part of your life that's offensive to the One you love the most, you surely want to know about it and deal with it.

My fear is that as our culture becomes more desensitized and shockproof, our consciences become looser and more self-justifying. We think, *Hey, times have changed, right? This thing in my life is no big deal—everybody does it now.* We're no longer alarmed by things we once recognized as sinful, harmful, and dangerous to our relationship with God and our own well-being. For this reason, I encourage you to ask God to keep you sensitive to sin, aware of his ways instead of just your own or our culture's.

Not only do you need to ask God for forgiveness each day, but you also need to make sure you're right with other people. Jesus basically said (in Matthew 6:14–15), "You'll be forgiven to the degree that you forgive other people." In the same way that you and I forgive each other, God forgives us. Pretty scary if you think about it! This means that it's vitally important to make deliberate decisions each day about how you're going to treat other people.

That's even true of people who've been mean to you—people who've been ugly, spiteful, or harmful. When you pray the way Jesus instructed, you're in effect saying, "God, those people who hurt me need to be forgiven in the same way I have been forgiven by you. So just as you've extended your mercy and forgiveness to me, I offer it to them as well. I want to forgive them, God, and let you take care of avenging and dealing with them wherever they are in their hearts. I'm not going to hold on to grudges, and I'm going to ask that they forgive me for how I've hurt them."

You're not only praying this for those offenses that have already taken place, but also for those that are yet to take place. It's an attitude, an overall approach to the world of being forgiving—or as I like to say, breath-giving. Instead of being fearful of all the mean, nasty, selfish people out in the world, you can show them the love of God because you know that he's big enough to handle their issues. You don't have to do God's job for him and monitor the gates to his kingdom.

When you let go of judging, condemning, and policing other people and their behavior, you'll discover that you have a lot more energy to devote to your real purpose: loving them and loving God. Paul writes, "Don't let evil conquer you, but conquer evil by doing good" (Romans 12:21 NLT).

You and I must make this decision every day. Otherwise, we

begin to feel hurt, offended, sinned against, and then justified for our own sinful behavior in return. Every day we should ask God to forgive us as we adopt a forgiving attitude toward the world.

SPIRITUAL WARFARE

Now we're ready to consider a critical part of the prayer that some people overlook: "and lead us not into temptation, but deliver us from evil." Let me first say that this traditional wording implies a different meaning from the original Greek text. It's more accurately expressed as "God, do not allow me to be led into temptation." It's important to realize that God does not lead us into temptation or set us up for failure. We're actually asking him to help us when temptation comes our way, to give us the power to resist and say no. Jesus is telling us that not only must we seek and grant forgiveness for what has happened in the past, but we must take our stand against the devil and ask God to help us resist his schemes against us in the future.

As we become more comfortable talking to God, we discover that there are different kinds of prayers. It's one thing to say a prayer of blessing or thanks before a meal or to offer a feel-good devotional. But we must also realize that we're in a war with our enemy, and sometimes warfare prayers are required. Scripture is clear about this: "Be strong in the Lord and in his mighty power. Put on the full armor of God, so that you can take your stand against the devil's schemes. . . . And pray in the Spirit on all occasions with all kinds of prayers" (Ephesians 6:10–11,18). It's not that we have to pray the right prayer so that God will listen, or that it works like some magic spell. We pray this way because we realize we're in the midst of a spiritual battle!

There are times for devotional prayer and other times when

confrontational prayer is necessary. We must renounce the unholy one and all his fiery arrows and crafty schemes. We must pray for protection around our families and friends, around our homes and churches. We need to consecrate and fortify our marriages and the lives of our children. We must take our stand against the forces of darkness in the name and power of Jesus Christ. Too often we think of prayer as a pleasant, dreamy meditation. But sometimes our prayers should be more like a street fight.

Maybe you're thinking, *Come on, Chris—is prayer really supposed to be that confrontational? Do we really need to be praying this way every day?* James 5:16 says, "The effectual fervent prayer of a righteous man availeth much" (KJV). When was the last time you prayed fervently? If you want to make a difference with your prayers, you can't just think of prayer as a time to sit and meditate on happy thoughts for ten minutes. At times, you and I need to confront the devil using the weapons God has given us.

GRAND FINALE

Finally, here are some instructions on ending our conversation time with God. Jesus tells us to put a big exclamation point at the end of it! "For thine is the kingdom, and the power, and the glory, for ever. Amen." We must have faith in God's ability to act. This part of the Lord's Prayer reminds us that God can do anything and that he's got everything he needs to accomplish his purposes in our lives.

When I conclude praying, I often like to end with this passage:

> This is the confidence we have in approaching God: that if we ask anything according to his will, he hears us. And if we know

> that he hears us—whatever we ask—we know that we have what we asked of him. (1 John 5:14–15)

What a great way to end, right? We have complete and total confidence in our Father, who can do everything he said he would do.

Though I grew up in church, I had no sense of the power of prayer. In fact, I figured it was just another thing Christians did to stay on God's good side. But as a teen attending Bethany World Prayer Center, which became my home church in Baton Rouge, I saw what it really looks like to worship God and pray. As I said earlier, Pastor Larry Stockstill led our church through twenty-one days of prayer to begin every year. It was during those seasons that I first witnessed the incredible power that God unleashes when his people join together to connect with him in prayer.

So it made sense that in January 2001—the month before Church of the Highlands held its first service—our launch team would spend twenty-one days seeking God together. And now, every January and August since, our church body has joined together again in 21 Days of Prayer, a time of praying (to connect with God) and fasting (to disconnect from the things of the world—whether it be certain foods, media, or anything that consumes too much of our time and attention).

During these intensive times of prayer, several thousand people meet at our various campuses every weekday morning for an hour of corporate worship and prayer. We're desperate to have God's strength and power behind everything we do, and we're grateful for the answers we've seen in response to this dedicated time of prayer.

If you have the opportunity to pray with other believers, I urge you to take it. Even if you don't, you can still follow Jesus's example.

Prayer is simply a conversation with God—spending time talking and listening to the One who made you and loves you most.

BREATHING LESSON

If you want to reinvigorate your conversations with God, I encourage you to make the Lord's Prayer your own. Take each of the seven phrases, putting the idea in your own words, then personalizing it.

Think about how you want to address God in a warm, loving way. Consider which of his names you want to remember and honor. Ask for his will to be done before your own agenda. And when you do ask for your needs to be met, invite God to meet them in all areas of your life, not just the urgent ones. Ask him for forgiveness, and ask him to help you forgive others in the same way.

Tell him you need him to help you avoid whatever tempts you personally. If you're tempted to go to the mall to shop and overspend, ask him to help you with that. If you're tempted to chat online with someone you shouldn't, ask him to be with you so that you don't go there. Whatever your temptation is, invite him to strengthen and fortify you. Take a stand against the enemy in your life.

And finally, have faith in God's ability to accomplish everything. This fresh-air approach will make prayer one of the most enjoyable parts of your day. Amen!

> Ask, and it will be given to you; seek, and you will find; knock, and it will be opened to you. For everyone who asks receives, and the one who seeks finds, and to the one who knocks it will be opened. What father among you, if his son asks for a fish, will instead of a fish give him a serpent;

or if he asks for an egg, will give him a scorpion? If you then, who are evil, know how to give good gifts to your children, how much more will the heavenly Father give the Holy Spirit to those who ask him!

—Luke 11:9–13 ESV

8

GOD'S LOVE LANGUAGE

A person will worship something. . . . Therefore, it behooves us to be careful what we worship, for what we are worshiping we are becoming.

RALPH WALDO EMERSON

When I was growing up, our family sometimes visited relatives, people from church, or friends from my father's work. My mom would always make sure we kids were all dressed appropriately, then give us a refresher course in etiquette. It didn't matter where we were going. She believed there were rules we should follow for how to behave once we were actually in someone's home.

This included how to respond if our hosts offered us refreshments or invited us to stay for lunch or supper. Every time we arrived at our destination, just as my father was pulling into the driveway, my mother would say, "Now, remember, if they offer you something to eat or drink, just say, 'No, thank you.'"

And, of course, I would ask, "But, Mom, what if I'm hungry?" Or, "Even if it's just something to drink?"

She would give me one of those mother-type looks that say far more than words can. "It's not polite," she'd answer. "Why not?" I'd say. "They're the ones offering." Getting a little exasperated (by now we were approaching our hosts' front door), she'd say, "They're just trying to be nice." After being welcomed inside, I'd be quiet. But in my mind, I always wondered: *Why would people just act nice by offering something they don't want to give us?*

Looking back, I realize my mom never wanted us to put anyone out, so she was essentially teaching her children a rote response to a polite question. It was just something we knew to say.

In fact, it reminded me of our Sunday morning worship services when the pastor would often say, "We thank the Lord because he has filled us with such joy." I'd always look around (and later, as a teenager, almost start laughing) because what I saw did not in any way resemble joy. Long faces and grim expressions. Downcast eyes and tightly clenched jaws. I had seen joy, and this definitely wasn't it. It just seemed to be a rote response.

SHOW YOUR FEELINGS

I actually liked and respected our pastor a great deal. Yet Sunday worship seemed to consist of either insincere expressions or words spoken or sung without any emotion. Maybe you experienced the same thing when you were young and watched most of the worshipers around you showing about as much enthusiasm as they might while waiting in their dentist's office for a root canal.

Growing up, I thought the world was way more fun than anything I'd seen in church. But based on what I understood about the Christian faith from reading the Bible and hearing our pastor preach, it should have been the opposite. I believed then—and I still maintain—that if we're connected to the living God who has forgiven our sins and provided a home in heaven for us, then it's truly the good news, the best news we'll ever hear.

Worship is love expressed. And it seems to me that if we've experienced this great news and encountered God's radical love, our expressions of love to him will resemble all the other love expressions in our life—not just the sincere love we have for our spouses or the dedicated love we have as parents, but even the unabashed enthusiasm we have for strawberry ice cream or the family dog.

Seriously, based on our expressions of love alone, some of us seem to love our dog more than God. And football? My goodness, don't even get me started about sports. Or enjoying good food? In case you've forgotten, I live in the South!

There's no doubt we all know how to worship; it's just a matter of where it's applied. This is true for all of us.

If we want to experience a breath of fresh air in every area of our lives, we must get a new perspective on what it means to worship God. When we do, we'll experience a blast of wind that will refresh and energize our relationship with him.

Worship is not what goes on in the church service, but what happens in individual hearts. Corporate worship is important, but love for God must be expressed throughout our lives—every day, in every way. That's what worship is all about.

THE LANGUAGE OF LONGING

Most people agree that worshiping God is a deeply personal issue. But I believe we miss the entire point when we reduce worship to nothing more than each person's subjective interpretation. If you ask people, "What's the proper expression of worship to God?" you'll likely end up with "Well, we all have our own way. There's your style, and my style—your tradition, and mine. You do it your way, I'll do it mine."

Let's challenge this idea. If worship is love expressed, it seems to me that we need to focus on what the object of our affection wants, not on what we personally like. If I'm going to love you, I can't just love you the way I want to love you; I have to love you the way you like being loved. Because of my love for you, I want to focus on you and offer you the things that meet your needs. So to say, "This is just my style or my preference or my tradition" for worshiping God doesn't seem to be a good starting point.

Thirty years ago, Gary Chapman wrote his book *The 5 Love Languages*, which remains a bestseller to this day.[1] As a pastor and professional counselor, Chapman wanted to help couples understand each other's needs so they could have stronger marriages. In the book, he describes five styles of giving and receiving love which he calls "love languages," and he explains how we can learn to speak in each other's primary love language.

One of these languages is grounded in acts of service. This happens to be my love language. If you do something for me, especially something I don't particularly enjoy doing for myself, this conveys love to me, more than physical affection or gifts. When my wife cooks my favorite meal or the kids surprise me with their voluntary yard work, I feel loved and appreciated.

My wife, on the other hand, really appreciates quality time together. Tammy doesn't care about all the other things as much, but if I just stop during the day and look into her eyes and ask, "Honey, how are you doing today?" she feels special. My willingness to give her some individual time in which I'm fully present and focused on what she needs speaks more than a dozen roses or a beautiful necklace (although I've never had her turn those down).

Speaking of flowers and jewelry, Chapman says that some people speak in the love language of gift giving. (Okay, I confess—I'm glad that's not Tammy's!) My son David is a "stuff" guy. All I have to do is give him something for him to feel loved. If he gets money for his birthday or Christmas, you can bet he'll be shopping online within twenty-four hours.

Another love language is spoken through words of affirmation. Some people don't want you to do anything for them or to give anything to them, and they don't necessarily need your time. But they do appreciate constant encouragement. They like to receive frequent feedback from the people around them on how they're doing. They feel loved when they receive the sincere compliments and honest affirmation of their loved ones.

My youngest son, Joseph, thrives on hearing these expressions of love from the rest of us. Our family has a birthday tradition where, during the birthday meal, we go around the table and tell some of the things we appreciate most about the birthday boy or girl. Joseph eats this up. I remember that at one birthday, he didn't even wait for his brother David to finish speaking before he turned to Michael and asked, "Okay, and what about you? What do you like about me?"

Another love language is physical touch or closeness. My daughter Sarah, who's now a young woman and taller than me, still loves to give and receive hugs. "Daddy, will you hold me?" is one of her favorite requests. We often think of people who speak this language as "touchy-feely," the huggers and shoulder patters who need physical closeness in order to feel loved and appreciated.

According to Dr. Chapman, the secret to becoming a great lover of people is learning their primary love language. If we're going to have a great marriage, a great relationship with our kids, or even productive relationships at work, we must discover those individuals' respective love languages and love them that way.

It seems to me that if we're going to love God in a way that he likes, we've got to know his love language. That means we must let go of focusing on worship as something to make us feel good. How often do we say, "Boy, I really enjoyed the worship service today!" or "I sure got a lot out of our worship time this morning"?

God's fresh air blows into our lives when we love him in the way he likes. *We don't worship for our benefit, but for his.*

FOR HIS PLEASURE

Scripture tells us (in Revelation 4:11) that God created us, along with all things, for his pleasure. Real worship, then, is not about us; it's about him. While God is not a human being, he displays emotions throughout the pages of Scripture. He grieves, gets jealous, becomes angry, and feels compassion, pity, sorrow, and sympathy. He loves, delights, rejoices, enjoys, and even laughs. All those expressions are in the Bible. We serve a God with emotions, a God who loves to be loved. We serve a God who has a love language and finds pleasure in our worship.

Throughout his Word he makes clear what his love language is, saying, "Here is what I like . . ." He reveals this for example throughout the Psalms, the longest book in Scripture. Likewise, when Jesus was asked to identify the greatest commandment, he replied, "Love the Lord your God" (Luke 10:27). If you think about it, loving God is the only thing we do now that we'll still be doing in heaven.

The word *praise* is used over and over in Scripture to describe what God desires. As we've seen, nuances of meaning can be lost when translating Hebrew and Greek text into English, and this seems especially true in regard to the biblical concept of *praise*.

In the Old Testament, when we read *praise* in our English Bible, it translates one of seven Hebrew words. Some of these are polar opposites of one another, yet all end up conveying the idea of *praise*. Let's consider each of these seven possibilities and their significance in how we worship God, as we seek to learn the specifics of God's love language. These seven meanings of *praise* can help us express our love in the ways he wants.

The first word, *hallel*, is used frequently in Scripture. It's where we get the word *hallelujah*. *Jah* means "God," so we're proclaiming, "*Hallel* God!" when we shout "Hallelujah!" *Hallel* means "to boast," "to rave," "to celebrate," and even "to be clamorously foolish."

If you've ever been to Tiger Stadium for an LSU football game, you might gain a deep appreciation for *hallel*. Just before the players run onto the field, masses of cheering fans in purple and gold yell, "Geaux Tigers!" The noise level kicks up another notch as the band plays the LSU fight song and the players run out onto the field. It's an exhilarating experience, and that's all just a warm-up for the excitement during the game itself.

You may be thinking, Really? Are you serious? God wants me to act like I do at a football game? I thought he wants me to be quiet and somber, with my eyes shut and head bowed. No, it's actually the opposite. "Those who seek the Lord will praise [hallel] him" (Psalm 22:26). God enjoys it when we hallel him. God enjoys it when we freely express our love and appreciation to him. Let's not worship a piece of leather more than we worship our living God.

The next word is *yadah*, which means to acknowledge someone or something in public with our hands extended. It literally means to raise our hands up toward heaven and acknowledge the greatness of God. This term is used in Psalm 138:1—"I will praise [*yadah*] you, Lord, with all my heart." Notice the way our bodies naturally express what we're feeling in our hearts—a longing, a reaching, a yearning to be closer. When we express our love to another person, our hands are almost always involved. This word *yadah* could be used to describe a child reaching up for his mommy or daddy while calling out, "Hold me!"

MORE OF WHAT GOD LIKES

The third word for praise in the Old Testament is *barak*. It's is used to convey blessing, giving thanks, bowing down, and even kneeling in humble gratitude. It's the opposite of our rowdy *hallel*-type praise. *Barak* means to honor God by presenting ourselves to him—to yield and say, "Here I am, Lord. I'm yours." It means I praise God by presenting my entire self to him: "Praise [*barak*] the Lord, my soul; all my inmost being" (Psalm 103:1). And we're told in 103:3–5 that when we give ourselves to the Lord as a *barak*-type praise offering, God forgives all our sin, heals all our diseases, redeems our lives from the pit, crowns us with love and compassion, and satisfies our desires with good things.

Next we find the Hebrew word *zamar*, which literally means to make music to God, or—to be more precise—to make music with stringed instruments before him. Music definitely seems to be a big part of God's love language.

And we don't necessarily have to like the music God likes. I don't listen to loud, jam-out, screamo music. I actually like (big secret!) classical music. If you check my playlist, you'll discover a lot of Beethoven and Mozart. Seriously. But what I like isn't necessarily all that God likes, so when I'm speaking his love language, I find something that I hope pleases him.

God likes it loud: "Praise him with the sounding of the trumpet, praise him with the harp and lyre, praise him with timbrel and dancing, praise him with the strings and pipe, praise him with the clash of cymbals, praise him with resounding cymbals" (Psalm 150:3–5). Notice the final repetition—God not only likes the clash of cymbals; he likes them resounding again and again!

The fifth word is *shabach.* Its meaning makes some people uncomfortable. It means to shout, to address in a loud tone, to holler. I like this one. If I go to a football game, I like to get loud and help pump up our team. And God likes it when we get loud and excited as we think about him. "Because your love is better than life, my lips will glorify you. I will praise [*shabach*] you as long as I live, and in your name I will lift up my hands" (Psalm 63:3–4). God's love language is audibly intense. He wants to hear us—and wants us to hear one another.

BETTER THAN FOOTBALL

Our sixth word, *towdah,* means to praise God by lifting our hands toward heaven in adoration. However, it's different from the kind of hand-raising denoted by *yadah. Towdah* describes lifting our hands in praise receptively, expectantly, waiting for things not yet received. While *yadah* implies us reaching up to God, *towdah* shows us receiving from God.

There's a sense of "Pour it on me, Lord, I'm ready. I'm here to bless you in your love language—but you keep giving it back because that's just who you are! You're a good God who gives good gifts. Thank you, Lord!"

In Scripture, we find this: "He who offers a sacrifice of thanksgiving [*towdah*] honors Me; and to him who orders his way aright I shall show the salvation of God" (Psalm 50:23 NASB).

Notice that two of the seven praise words involve lifting our hands. If people give you a hard time for having your hands up when you worship publicly, just tell them that you're talking to God in his love language.

The final Hebrew word for "praise" is *tehilah*. It means exuberant singing. "I will extol the LORD at all times; his praise [*tehilah*] will always be on my lips" (Psalm 34:1).

Think about the picture these praise words create when combined: acting clamorously foolish, with hands lifted, playing loud instruments, shouting, and singing exuberantly. Sounds more like an Alabama–Auburn game or a reunion between family members at the airport than the worship at most church services. Wouldn't it be great if Sunday mornings at church were more exciting than Saturday afternoons at the stadium?

WHO'S ON FIRST?

The truth is, each of us is likely practicing these seven kinds of worship already; there's something we're exuberant about, lifting our hands in excitement over, and probably getting loud and passionate about from time to time. You're worshiping something or someone now. It's already happening. So the question isn't *whether* you are a worshiper, but *what* or *whom* are you worshiping? Where are we directing our praise?

Maybe the place to begin getting fresh air in your worship life is not by changing your style of worship but by changing its direction. If your expressions of love go to your dog, your spouse, your football, your house, your hunting, or your shopping, you're worshiping that person or thing more passionately than God. I'm not saying you can't get excited about your family, your hobbies, or even your possessions. It's just a matter of whether those other things you love reflect God's goodness to you, or take his place.

God doesn't want to be a second-rate love in your life. Since he mentions it in the first commandment—"You shall have no other gods before me" (Exodus 20:3)—it's clearly important to him that he come first in your life. Jesus said it this way: "Love the Lord your God with all your heart, all your soul, all your mind, and all your strength" (Mark 12:30 NLT). He said this was "the most important commandment" (verse 29).

Jesus here basically gives us a worship checkup. These are three areas, he said, that should be focused foremost on loving God. First, we should love him with all our heart and soul. How do we do that? If we worship anything with our heart and soul, we give it our affections,[2] which means we express our love in clear, passionate ways. Some people have told me, "I do worship God passionately. I just do it privately, in my heart." If I told my wife something like that . . . well, you can imagine how it would go over. "Honey, I love you, but don't expect hugs or kisses. I love you in my heart, but I don't hug." That wouldn't go over too well. God wants our affection. If we're capable of worshiping only "in our hearts," we're withholding ourselves from the One we say we love most.

HEART AND SOUL

If you look in the Bible, it's clear that a lot of people understood this. David got it. He wrote, "I would rather be a gatekeeper in the house of my God than live the good life in the homes of the wicked" (Psalm 84:10 NLT). Essentially he was saying, "I would do anything to be around you, God." Now, David made some huge mistakes in his life and yet God called him "a man after my own heart." God always showed favor to David because David got it. He was a worshiper; he expressed his love. He wrote love poetry to God, he played music for God, he danced for God.

Too often, many of us seem afraid to let go and let our love loose before God. We've allowed what people think about us determine our expression to God. So when we worship God, we look around to see who might be watching, or we base our worship on what everyone else is doing. We focus on our own feelings instead of God's.

I encourage you to go for it. Let yourself get excited about God and your relationship with him. Allow yourself to love him in his love language, in the ways that he says are special to him. Love him with all your heart and soul.

The second way Jesus asks us to love God, after worshiping with our whole heart and soul, is to worship God with our minds. How in the world do we worship God with our minds? We simply focus our thoughts on God. Consider the way our minds work when we're falling in love with someone. Our beloved is the last one we think about before we go to sleep. He or she is the one we dream about. That person is in our waking thoughts. God wants to preoccupy our minds in the same way.

Whatever you worship, you think about most of the time. If you love golf, you're often thinking, *I wonder if I can fit in a little time at the driving range this afternoon?* If you love shopping, you frequently wonder, *What time do those stores close?* If you love football, you know exactly how many days until the season begins. If you go to the website of your favorite team (I confess I go to mine every day), you are likely to find a clock counting down the days, hours, and minutes until next season's kickoff. I haven't met anyone, myself included, who has that kind of counter showing how long until the next worship service.

I remember a time when I was reading in my home office and my son Jonathan came in. He was sixteen at the time, and already tall—over six feet—and strong. I looked up and smiled and said, "Hey, buddy, what do you need?" He looked back at me and said, "Nothing. I just thought I'd hang out with you a little while. Was just thinking about you, Dad."

Talk about making an old dad feel all mushy inside! How cool is that? My teenage son was thinking about me and just wanted to come and be with me with no real agenda. The message I received is that he loves me. He didn't want anything from me at that time other than to be with me. The Lord revealed something to me during that time with Jonathan. God whispered to me, "Chris, this is worship. And I like it when you just want to be near me. When you just think about me throughout your day, regardless of where you are or what you're doing."

ALWAYS ON MY MIND

So here's the checkup: Certain people, topics, and events will predominate your thoughts today, tonight, tomorrow, the rest of this week, and for weeks to come. What do you think about most? What are you thinking about right now? Is it God?

You know that experience you have when you're planning a really great vacation that's long overdue? It may be months away, but your plane tickets are bought, your spouse is already shopping for beachwear for the whole family, and you're all excited just knowing it's coming up. As it gets closer and closer, you think about it more and more. God wants to be on our minds in the same way. He doesn't care if we love golf or look forward to a vacation. He does mind it, though, if he's not on the top of our list.

Finally, Jesus told us to worship God with all of our strength. Every day when people from our congregation volunteer hours of their time to feed people, pass out clothing, refurbish homes, and provide a host of other practical expressions of love for God through the Birmingham Dream Center, God receives it all as worship.

So when you're greeting people at the door of the church on Sundays or leading a small group or showing generosity to a person in need, you're worshiping. When you're using your gifts to build something, bake something, sew something, create something in service to God and his kingdom, you're expressing your love to him. This is why I never want anyone at our church to feel pressured or obligated to serve in any way. If someone isn't able to offer what they do as a gift of worship, they shouldn't do it.

My wife likes it when I'm affectionate and show her how much I love her, but she also wants to see how much I love her when I'm out in the backyard mowing the lawn. She needs me to be a yard boy just as much as a lover boy!

How you treat the people you love reflects your feelings and expresses your devotion to them. How you expend your human energy and physical strength is a good indicator of what you love. What do you spend most of your time doing? Are you doing it for God? Or for someone or something else?

BREATHING LESSON

If you want to experience a breath of fresh air, a real life-giving burst, be willing to worship God in all the ways he appreciates. Examine your affections, your thoughts, and your activities to see where you're directing them. Whatever excites you most in life—sports or traveling or spending time with family—should pale in comparison to how passionate you are about God.

I encourage you to step outside your comfort zone and worship God in the ways the Bible describes—heartfelt and full of expression. When you do so, you're letting him and everyone around you know how much you love him. And the result? Well, just try it and see how he refreshes you in return.

> The trumpeters and singers performed together in unison to praise and give thanks to the LORD. Accompanied by trumpets, cymbals, and other instruments, they raised their voices and praised the LORD with these words: "He is good! His faithful love endures forever!" At that moment a thick cloud filled the Temple of the LORD.
>
> —2 Chronicles 5:13 NLT

9

WHERE EVERYBODY KNOWS YOUR NAME

Friendship is born at that moment when one person says to another, "What! You too? I thought I was the only one."

C. S. LEWIS

A few years ago, Tammy and I were in China on a church mission trip. Our group decided to spend our last day sightseeing. We spent the morning at the Great Wall of China—what an amazing place! It was definitely spectacular.

Because I needed to be back in the States before the rest of the group, Tammy and I had to return to the airport before everyone else. I explained the situation to our friends, then Tammy and I headed back to where we had started the tour. We were already in a cab when I heard someone shouting my name. "Chris! Chris! Over here—you have to see this!"

It was our tour director, a missionary who knew the language and culture quite well. Since we were worried about the time, I said, "Sorry, but we've really got to go—our flight's in only a few hours." We went back and forth like this until he insisted, "Now, I won't take no for an answer. I really have to show you and Tammy something that you absolutely don't want to miss. Grab your bags. You can get going after you see this!"

Annoyed, I let out a big sigh. We grabbed our luggage and trudged over to see what was worth risking being late for our flight. Once I was next to him, the tour director said quietly, "Chris, that wasn't a real cab! It's one of those look-alikes where the driver takes you out into the country, beats the life out of you, steals everything you have, and leaves you for dead. I had to get you out of there without the driver knowing I was on to him." You can imagine how incredibly grateful Tammy and I were to this man for probably saving our lives. He had our backs when we didn't even know we were in danger.

STOPPING SHORT

Each of us needs other people just as much as my wife and I needed someone watching our backs as we prepared to head to the airport in China. For many of us, however, relationships seem just as threatening as a robber waiting to mug us in a back alley. Nothing has the potential to drain our breath and leave us feeling alone and exhausted more than other people. The hurts, the wounds, the bad relationships that drain us of life and breath and energy begin to take a toll and affect all the other areas of our lives. Most people are wounded, and this may be the single greatest area that prevents us from reaching our full potential.

One of the most overlooked stories in the Bible is that of Terah, the father of our great father in the faith, Abraham. This man also experienced a painful loss that ended up preventing him from reaching his intended destination:

> This is the account of Terah's family line. Terah became the father of Abram, Nahor and Haran. And Haran became the father of Lot. While his father Terah was still alive, Haran died in Ur of the Chaldeans, in the land of his birth. (Genesis 11:27–28)

In the next verses, we see God trying to move in Terah's life, trying to get him to Canaan, the Promised Land. In fact, I wonder if God's original call was to Terah, not Abraham:

> Terah took his son Abram, his grandson Lot son of Haran, and his daughter-in-law Sarai, the wife of his son Abram, and together they set out from Ur of the Chaldeans to go to Canaan. But when they came to Harran, they settled there. Terah lived 205 years, and he died in Harran. (Genesis 11:31–32)

Although this family moved from their native land toward Canaan, the land of milk and honey, Terah never made it there. Perhaps when he and his family reached a city that just so happened to have almost the same name as his dead son, he could go no farther.

Terah had to pass through Harran in order to go where God

was calling him. Once there, I suspect that he must have been reminded of his pain. And he just stopped. He couldn't go on. It was too hard, too painful, too demanding. It seems he could not let go of his grief in order to embrace the joy that lay ahead. He likely could not believe that God was still in control and had not abandoned him. He stopped short based on his own perceptions, rather than pursuing the truth of God's destination. As a result, he never reached the place God wanted to take him.

Like Terah, many of us are shaped by our negative experiences and never overcome them to discover the destiny to which God is calling us. Too often we stop short, refusing to believe we can catch our breath and enjoy an abundant life. We succumb to fears and false perceptions. The enemy defeats us with lies that bog us down, causing us to lose energy and hope. We get stuck in the doldrums, a dead zone from which we just can't seem to emerge and get back on track.

BAGGAGE CLAIM

Life should come with one of those big signs that you see on ocean beaches, the kind that cautions swimmers to beware of riptides. Only this one would read, "Warning: When we're hurt, we're not very smart." Pain can cause blindness and obstruct objectivity and common sense. Things may look calm on the surface, but a swirling vortex below waits to swallow us up. We let the past define the future and never move on. We think we're doing the right thing, but often we're simply doing whatever alleviates our pain in some way. When we reach debilitating places, as the land of Harran was for Terah, we must allow ourselves to need and to trust the people in our lives.

Certainly, the enemy's lies pollute our other relationships. Terah's decision affected his whole family. In Genesis 12, we see that God had to separate the family. He called Abraham to move on, leave his father's house, and follow God's leading. What an incredibly difficult decision that must have been.

The problem with baggage is that it affects other people's trips. Have you ever been traveling with a group and had one person's lost luggage impact everyone on the tour? You're traveling together, perhaps for a work convention, a church mission trip, a school field trip, or just a vacation with friends. Almost everyone packs light and reduces their luggage to a carry-on. And yet there's the one person who checks two bags and still drags an overstuffed duffel on board. It's bad enough that the entire group has to wait at baggage claim upon arrival, but if just one person's luggage gets lost, it causes delays, frustrations, and disappointment for everyone.

The same is true for us. The more baggage we carry, the more it slows us down. And our relationships are affected when we can't handle our own issues and constantly force everyone else to deal with them too. Our wounds get transferred to the people close to us. And unless they're vigilant and know how to handle us, our pain becomes contagious and compounds our heartache.

We make decisions that aren't good for us and create defense systems to ensure that we're never hurt in the same way again. We become controlling and rigid, suspicious and skeptical of others' motives. Our insecurities accumulate from an ocean wave into a tsunami of paranoia, fear, and distrust.

The most tragic result of unresolved pain is that it can destroy our relationship with God. After Abram moves on, Terah is never heard from again. His story ends there.

NEVER WALK ALONE

God actually intended people to be a source of life, a community of support and fellowship, taking care of one another. As I shared earlier, I'm fascinated by Paul's shout-out to his friend Onesiphorus, whom he described as a breath of fresh air (2 Timothy 1:16 TLB).

I gained a new appreciation for this kind of friendship when I was preparing to plant Church of the Highlands in 2001. The first thing I did was assemble a team of people who wanted to help me. I called this committed team of thirty-four people the launch team. John Maxwell once said that "it takes teamwork to make the dream work."[1] That's so true. None of us could have even come close to accomplishing individually what we accomplished together. Our shared vision, commitment, and devotion made us better together.

Genuine fellowship—that sense of having a few people in our lives who really know us, accept us, and love us—can make all the difference in the world. A sense of community can make our trials bearable and our triumphs worth celebrating. We can listen and share, help and encourage, support and be supported.

When we aren't in community, we can quickly find ourselves drifting into the doldrums again. "Let us . . . not give up meeting together, as some are in the habit of doing, but encouraging one another—and all the more as you see the Day approaching" (Hebrews 10:24–25). This is not just talking about attending church or even being part of a small group or Bible study. We can attend any gathering of people and still be lonely. We can be surrounded by people and yet feel totally isolated, withholding our hearts and not receiving what others want to offer us.

Throughout the Bible, we consistently see the importance of being part of a group of people with whom we can be open and honest. Today, most churches call them small groups or community groups, and emphasize their importance as the lifeblood of their body. Nonetheless, many of us still walk alone, tripping and limping along instead of walking lockstep on our faith journeys with fellow pilgrims.

Walking alone never works. As much as we want to be self-sufficient and independent, the truth is that we can't find lasting satisfaction in ourselves. We can earn all the money in the world and achieve all kinds of amazing feats, but if we don't have others to share our success with, we're just as empty as we were before we were flush with money and accomplishments. "There was a man all alone; he had neither son nor brother. There was no end to his toil, yet his eyes were not content with his wealth" (Ecclesiastes 4:8).

LONE RANGERS

Since most of us would agree that we need others, why do so many of us try to go it alone? I'm guessing that as soon as you read that question, a dozen reasons immediately sprang to your mind. I'm also guessing that some are legitimate and others are just excuses. Let's think through some of these reasons together and explore ways to move beyond them and experience the intimate connections we all crave.

First, there's naivete. Some people just assume that they must face life alone, and so they never take time to build meaningful relationships. Having never tasted true love and support, the genuine encouragement of other people, they remain independent and naively believe they don't need anyone. Many may even develop a tough exterior and try to bulldoze over the people around them. So often, though, that toughness overlooks the fundamental human need we all have for other people.

There's a story about legendary boxer Muhammad Ali in his heyday, flying to one of his matches. As the flight attendant went through the safety procedures, she noticed that Ali didn't have his seat belt fastened. The attendant told him it was mandatory that all passengers be buckled in before takeoff, but still the famous fighter would not comply. He said, "Superman doesn't need a seat belt!" To which the quick-witted flight attendant responded, "Superman doesn't need an airplane either!"

Another reason many people often try to go it alone is because of their temperament. We may blame ourselves and think we're just not cut out to be part of the group because we aren't very outgoing. We avoid those settings where we have to meet new people, telling ourselves, *That's just the way I am.*

We convince ourselves that others just won't understand us or accept us. We decide we're not very interesting. The truth, however, is that others are often much more accepting of us than we are of ourselves. We end up condemning ourselves for a variety of reasons, then lose all perspective on what's true and real. If we'll let them, other people can be truth bearers and remind us of God's grace, love, and compassion.

FEAR FACTOR

This leads us to another major barrier: fear. It never gets easier to risk sharing who we are and what we feel unless we practice doing it. As a pastor, I've discovered that no matter how often we talk about the benefits of joining a small group, some people remain intimidated by the thought of it. They imagine sitting in a chair in the middle of the room while everyone grills them and picks them apart. They're afraid they'll be put on the spot and exposed for who they really are. And ultimately, like all of us, they're afraid they won't be loved. They believe that others will reject them if they really get to know them.

This fear is often based on past experiences where in fact we were rejected, abandoned, or abused by other people. Many of us have been burned in the past, and the effects can linger many years after the offense—so much so that we vow to ourselves we will never let that happen to us again. We commit to never needing anyone and never allowing ourselves to be vulnerable and transparent for fear of showing our weaknesses, for fear of revealing things that will be used against us.

This fear of telling others our secrets reminds me of a men's group I heard about. These three guys were good friends and had been meeting for prayer and Bible study for a while, but each had a secret. As they got to know one another over time, one guy finally said, "Guys, I've got to tell you something. I'm really wrestling with lust and looking at online porn. It's just so easy to click and find it anytime. I really need your prayers and your help in defeating this habit."

The second guy said, "Wow, I really appreciate your honesty—thanks for being real. Since you were, I might as well tell you guys the truth as well. I'm a gambling addict, and I've put my family in serious debt. I take huge risks on the stock market, play online poker, and go to the casino every chance I get. I need your help to beat the odds and overcome this thing."

The third guy looked at his two friends and said, "Well, guys, I'll confess as well. I really struggle with gossip, and I can't wait until I get out of here!"

Seriously, most of us fear that someone will tell our secrets and betray our confidence. We're terrified of what people might think if we reveal our darkest struggles. It just seems so much safer not to let people know. They'll only betray us, right? So why put ourselves in that position when we can just keep them at arm's length by smiling and saying, "I'm just fine—and how are you?"

There's a reason that our enemy attacks our relationships. He knows wounds caused by others can be some of the harshest, most debilitating injuries we'll ever face. Being betrayed by another person is absolutely one of the worst things that we can experience. Whether that betrayal comes from a parent or a teacher, from a best friend's gossiping tongue or from the keyboard of our spouse's laptop, we feel crushed and powerless. Pain is part of every relationship, but we get to choose whether it's the deadening pain of separation or the growing pains of reconciliation.

NONE OF YOUR BUSYNESS

Another reason we give for going it alone is busyness. We say, "Well, of course I'd love to have closer relationships and more time for family and friends. There's just so much going on right now. Maybe when things settle down . . ." But they never settle down, do they? We've let the world set the agenda for us.

In our overstimulated world, which bombards us with constant information, entertainment, and education opportunities, we can always point to something we feel obligated to do. So many of us paralyze ourselves in the doldrums because we're tired and burned out from overwork and only rarely allow ourselves to relax and unplug. When we're busy, we wish we could slow down. But when we try to slow down, our minds are preoccupied with all the work we've left undone, all the things waiting for us when we return. So we bounce back and forth like Ping-Pong balls, never experiencing rest or the soul refreshment that real relationships can give us.

While I love social media and appreciate the ways it allows us to communicate and connect, I also fear that it gives us a false sense of relationship. We post what we want others to see on social media, we text, we email and chat, but we don't slow down long enough to sit across from people so we can look them in the eye and listen to their hearts. We don't slow down enough to reveal ourselves to them in person.

If you're serious about wanting fresh air in your life, I encourage you to reprioritize your life as necessary to make authentic relationships a deliberate commitment on your part. Charles Swindoll summed it up well:

> Nobody is a whole team. . . . We need each other. You need someone and someone needs you. Isolated islands we're not. To make this thing called life work, we've got to lean and support. Relate and respond. Give and take. Confess and forgive. Reach out and embrace. Since none of us is a whole, independent, self-sufficient, super-capable, all-powerful hotshot, let's quit acting like we are. Life's lonely enough without our playing that silly role. The game is over. Let's link up."[2]

CHEERS

God never intended for us to walk through life alone. And deep down, we know it. When the Lord saw that Adam was alone in the garden, he observed that it is not good for man to be alone. So he created Eve, and from them came the first family, the first community. And yes, just like us, they had their issues after making the fateful choice to bite the apple of disobedient discontent. But our longing for connection, for friendship, for relationship, is still inside us—a foundational part of every human being.

Do you remember the classic sitcom *Cheers*, set in a Boston tavern? Its theme song articulates a very simple message that clearly resonates with us all: "Sometimes you want to go where everybody knows your name, and they're always glad you came. . . . You wanna go where everybody knows your name."[3] We want to be known and recognized. We want a place where we belong. We want to be able to trust other people and know that they relate to us without judgment. We want to experience relationships that give us life and put our problems in perspective.

It seems to me that the place where we can find a supportive community should be our local church, not the corner bar. Unfortunately, there's often more joy, support, fellowship, and encouragement in a neighborhood pub than in a church small group.

This is not the way God intended it to be. There should be more acceptance, more safety, more encouragement in our relationships with other believers than anywhere else.

Since the beginning of Church of the Highlands, we've deliberately created a place where knowing your name is a priority for everyone. We've been more than a church with big weekend services. We've been a church made up of small groups of people doing life together.

Whether they meet in homes, parks, restaurants, college dorm rooms, or offices, these groups form the heart and soul of who we are as the body of Christ. By the way, these groups aren't intended to be just another church event, something to fill a slot on people's calendars. Our vision is for everyone to be part of a group with other individuals who are willing to grow in their faith together, to support one another, to encourage one another, and to celebrate with one another.

Such groups reflect Paul's desire for believers: "So it is with Christ's body. We are many parts of one body, and we all belong to each other" (Romans 12:5 NLT). We need people in our lives who are willing to share in the good and the bad, the ups and the downs.

In the second year of our church, a man in one of our small groups had cancer and lost all his hair to chemo. While the group members offered all kinds of practical support, one of the most moving things the other men did was to shave their heads too. They wanted their friend to know they were standing with him.

No one should have to deal with a disease like cancer alone. No one should have to sit in a hospital waiting room alone while their spouse or child or parent is in surgery. No one should have to wait for test results to a biopsy alone. No one should have to stand at an open grave alone. No one should have to go through a divorce alone. We need each other.

NEIGHBORHOOD WATCH

Years ago, our church brought in someone to lead our staff through the DISC personality assessment. Before we took the test, the presenter taught us about four aspects of our interactions with other people. The first is the public face we put forward, how others see us and how we see ourselves. If we were to describe this part of ourselves, we might say, "I know and you know." This is the face we all see.

But allowing others into our lives is scary and challenging and intimidating. So we create the second aspect—masks, areas of our lives where "I know but you don't know." We all have those parts of ourselves that no one knows. Our secrets. Our past hurts and wounds and scars. Our deepest fears and insecurities. Our special hopes and dreams. While we think it feels safer to walk alone than to reveal these parts of ourselves, the truth is that we're never safe if no one knows us.

But living life with a mask on doesn't work. This is why Paul writes, "We refuse to wear masks and play games. . . . Rather, we keep everything we do and say out in the open" (2 Corinthians 4:2 MSG). Removing our masks is one of the secrets to getting rid of habitual sin. Certainly, God forgives us our sins, but in order to find healing we need to let someone else know too. We're told, "Confess your sins to each other and pray for each other so that you may be healed" (James 5:16 NLT).

We all need the kind of accountability where others are watching over our souls and we're watching out for them. Not so we can all become self-righteous chaperones policing each other's behavior, but so we can get our sin outside ourselves and see its effect on our lives and on the lives of others. When no one knows what we are doing, we're not safe.

We tell ourselves that we can be anonymous, that no one will get hurt, that no one will find out. But whatever we do secretly—whether it's drinking or stealing or watching porn or going places we shouldn't go—separates us from God and other people. And this separation will only grow the longer we keep our secrets.

As the saying goes, "You're only as sick as your secrets." If we want to be healthy and whole, if we want fresh air in our lives, someone needs to know what's really going on in our lives. Much of the time, we need the protection of others more than we even realize.

When we go on vacation, many of us ask someone to watch our

house, maybe even to house-sit. We want someone to protect our possessions, to take care of our pets, and to maintain our obligations. How much more, then, do we need others who will watch out for our souls as we travel through life? Real community provides a neighborhood watch for the soul.

SEEING THE BLIND SIDE

My wife and I have signals we use between us when we're together in public. You know, in case one of us has spinach in his teeth or needs a tissue for her nose. That's a good illustration of the third aspect of our lives: those things we don't know about ourselves but others do. Even though we think we know ourselves well, even the most self-aware person can't see their own blind spots. No matter how polite, how well-educated, how fit, how wealthy, or how charming each of us may be, we still can never fully know ourselves.

Our enemy loves to exploit our blind spots: to tempt us, shame us, frustrate us, trip us up. Every day he's devising ways to get us to fail. We usually don't recognize him, because if we did, we would flee into our Father's arms. Instead, the devil waits for us to turn our backs, to look the other way, to get preoccupied with other distractions so he can attack us where we're most vulnerable. His attempts usually work best when we're trying to go it alone. A wolf won't attack an entire flock of sheep. No, he waits for a straggler; a loner; a weaker, slower lamb who's fallen behind.

The reality is that we need people to be honest with us. Think about this for a moment. Who is speaking into your life with total and complete honesty? Telling you things that are hard to hear, what they know you may not want to hear? It has to be someone you trust, or else you'll dismiss that person's observations or insights. And in order for trust to grow, you have to be committed over time to helping each other. "Faithful are the wounds of a friend, but the kisses of an enemy are deceitful" (Proverbs 27:6 NKJV).

JOIN THE TEAM

Finally, there's the aspect of our untapped potential. This is the part of us that we can't see and that others can't see. Only God sees it. He alone knows what's inside us, and he wants us to mature and grow and develop into all that he created us to be. All of us have unrealized potential, and we will never reach our full potential alone. We need others to help us discover and utilize all the gifts we've been given. My potential as a pastor was never realized until I discovered my team. You'll always do more and accomplish more as part of a team.

Golf is a lonely sport—just you and the course. But there's a game you can play with a team called "Scramble." Each foursome gets to choose which player's shot they will count. Then they all hit from that spot for the next stroke. Each player contributes in the area of his or her strength—whether hitting from the tee or putting—and each one benefits from the others' strengths. An old Zambian proverb sums it up well: "When you run alone, you run fast. But when you run together, you run far."

Who's on your team? Who knows your dreams? Who knows you well enough to glimpse your potential as it emerges? Who can nurture and encourage you for the distance so you become the person you were meant to be? We need people who will help grow us into who we really are.

Jesus certainly modeled this kind of selective relational

investment by choosing only twelve disciples. He didn't want to start a religious movement or go on a world tour. He chose twelve other men, none of them anywhere near perfect, and shared with them his life, his heart, and his love of God. He wants us to pursue the same kind of intimacy today. He wants us to bring a breath of fresh air to every relationship we have and, in turn, to be refreshed ourselves.

BREATHING LESSON

God created you to draw support from others and to be a source of life to other people. But you need more than just another dozen friends on social media or another handful who follow you on Instagram. You need more than just the people at the office in the cubicles around you. You need more than just the guys you work out with or the ladies in your book club.

Whether you like it or not, God's plan to keep you out of the doldrums involves other people. He wants you to connect to him and to his people. To do so, you'll need to move past Harran (your past hurts and disappointments) and develop meaningful relationships. You'll never fully get the wind back in your sails until you do.

Take a moment to assess the relationships in your life. Who really knows you? Who gets you? What risks do you need to take and what secrets do you need to share in order to improve the quality of your relationships? Certainly, you want to be discerning and thoughtful about which people you trust. The integrity of your friends is far more important than the number of friends you have.

> A man of many companions may come to ruin, but there is a friend who sticks closer than a brother.
>
> —Proverbs 18:24 (ESV)

10

MONEY MATTERS

Money never made a man happy yet, nor will it.
The more a man has, the more he wants.
Instead of filling a vacuum, it makes one.

BENJAMIN FRANKLIN

My dad was my hero. He was the best man at my wedding. He was instrumental in helping me start Church of the Highlands here in Birmingham. After a brave battle with cancer, he went to be with the Lord on June 29, 2010. I miss him more than any words can describe.

My dad made his living as a numbers guy, serving as a legislative auditor for the State of Louisiana for most of his career. He retired in his mid-fifties with full retirement benefits after his decades of service. In 2000, when I announced that I was moving to Birmingham to plant a church, he and Mom decided it was time to make their own announcement. After talking about it for a while, they had decided to move from Baton Rouge too. They were going to buy a recreational vehicle and spend the rest of their lives traveling the country, living in America's most beautiful parks as "full-timers," as such nomads are called in the RV world.

My parents decided their first stop would be Birmingham so they could help me launch the church and set up its financial systems and controls before they moved on. Dad and Mom parked their RV at Oak Mountain State Park just outside Birmingham and served seven days a week as accountant and secretary for the newly formed church. However, they never made it out of Alabama. Mom and Dad fell in love with Birmingham and Church of the Highlands and never visited another park. They sold their RV, bought a home in Birmingham, and continued to serve our church.

My dad was a financial genius. The systems and controls he set up for our church were done through the lens of an auditor—not an accountant or attorney. Auditors see things differently. They make sure every *i* is dotted and every *t* is crossed. Dad implemented values and practices that God honored and our people appreciated. To many people who had attended other churches, his financial integrity was like a breath of fresh air.

Dad always taught me that God's heart is that of a giver—just think of John 3:16. It was natural, then, for us to model generosity at the Highlands from the beginning. That is why we give away everything—T-shirts, notebooks, coffee mugs, etc. We tell our congregation that they can't buy these things because they already paid for them through their tithes and offerings.

It has also been important to our leadership team that we gain the respect of our people by leveraging the money they give. Rather than simply giving to missions, for instance, we have joined with other congregations to plant churches that also give to missions.[1] Partnering together, we've been able to contribute millions of dollars—far more than our church could have given on our own.

My father's influence is evident in many more practices at Church of the Highlands. His dedication was unbelievable, even after being diagnosed with cancer in 2008. While he battled the cancer that had developed in a tumor on the side of his head, just behind his right eye, he never missed a day of work. Even through thirty-seven rounds of radiation, he remained positive, hopeful, and productive. He was brave, honest, and the hardest-working person I've ever met. His legacy and the lessons he deposited live on in my life and in the life of each person who is touched by our church.

PRINCIPLE, NOT PRESSURE

As I reflect back on the many nuggets of wisdom from my dad, one seems to sum up his entire approach to life. Dad always said, "Live by principle—not pressure." The result of that wisdom in his own life, in our family, and in our church was more than evident. There was freedom—a wind in the sails of his life that transported all of us to a fuller, richer, more faith-filled existence.

From my experience, most people can't say that about their lives, especially in the areas of money and time. The world persuades us to spend money we don't have and invest time in pursuits that bring us only temporary satisfaction. We often have little left over in time or money for either God or our family, and our relationships feel stagnant or strained as a result.

So many of us are on financial life support, barely making ends meet and holding our breath every month to see if we have enough to pay the bills and meet our expenses. Our financial lives end up leaving us like someone struggling with asthma; we're gasping for air and laboring over each breath:

> Give careful thought to your ways. You have planted much, but harvested little. You eat, but never have enough. You drink, but never have your fill. You put on clothes, but are not warm. You earn wages, only to put them in a purse with holes in it. (Haggai 1:5–6)

Money is one of the greatest sources of pain and anxiety in our lives—not only on an individual level, but also on a community, state, national, and global level. We see all kinds of financial unrest, from collapsed economies of entire countries to the economic recessions that occasionally plague our own nation. People want solutions; they want change and a new way of dealing with the issues of debt, credit, wealth, and poverty.

And it makes sense that people are tired of the way money matters control their lives. Basically, when it comes to money, we're not free—we're in bondage. We're in trouble as a nation. We're in trouble around the world. We have more abundance than ever before in history and yet we're less satisfied. The toll of worry, stress, and anxiety that millions of people experience because they're in debt up to their eyeballs only continues.

PIERCING PROSPERITY

Certainly, these problems didn't happen overnight. It's a cycle going on for generations. Every culture fights for their freedom, and once freedom is achieved, the by-product is prosperity. As I see it, this is where the problem begins. Most people don't know how to handle material abundance.

Prosperity stirs up greed. Statistically, it's been demonstrated that the more a person's income increases, the less they give away. Shouldn't it be the other way around? Yes, there are certainly wealthy, generous individuals who give away healthy percentages of their net worth, but most people become greedier when they make more money. They get ahead, but it's never enough.

We also reach into the future to have more now. Many people continue to borrow more and more, spending far beyond their income. Consumer borrowing rates fall during economic downturns, but quickly shoot back up when the economy improves.[2] We go from freedom to prosperity, from prosperity to greed, then from greed to bondage. We're miserable and feel trapped, on an endless treadmill from which there seems to be no escape.

And this is not a new phenomenon. Scripture describes this cycle in a way that's as timely as any headline you see in the news:

> Godliness with contentment is great gain. For we brought nothing into the world, and we can take nothing out of it. But if we have food and clothing, we will be content with that. Those who want to get rich fall into temptation and a trap and into many foolish and harmful desires that plunge people into ruin and destruction. For the love of money is a root of all kinds of evil. Some people, eager for money, have wandered from the faith and pierced themselves with many griefs. (1 Timothy 6:6–10)

We're trapped by our faulty decisions, blinded by a desire to have all we want right now, no matter what it steals from our future.

To experience a breath of fresh air in our finances, it's time for a new way of thinking. We must cultivate an attitude of contentment and maintain practices that give life.

My father taught me four values and three complementary practices, all based on God's Word, that can move you out of your financial storm and into calm waters. These values and their applications can put wind in your sails once again.

FULL DISCLOSURE

The first value is integrity. You must be willing to take an honest look in the mirror and make a truthful inventory. The process of change begins with your own personal disciplines:

> This, then, is how you ought to regard us: as servants of Christ and as those entrusted with the mysteries God has revealed. Now it is required that those who have been given a trust must prove faithful. (1 Corinthians 4:1–2)

A healthy financial culture begins with each individual—with each person's firm foundation based on integrity, not on greed and deceit. God knows how you handle your finances behind closed doors. Other people are watching as well. Regardless of the spin you might place on your decisions, your actions show what you value. That's why the apostle Paul said:

> We want to avoid any criticism of the way we administer this liberal gift. For we are taking pains to do what is right, not only in

the eyes of the Lord but also in the eyes of man. (2 Corinthians 8:20–21)

Think about it this way. If your family's expenditures for the year were printed for the public to see, what would embarrass you the most? How would you feel if everybody knew about your personal budget, debt, and giving? Most people would be embarrassed about some area of their finances if it were made public.

The same applies to churches and other organizations. Often, people want to be more generous, but they grow skeptical and cynical about how the resources they give are being used. They want the methods and purposes used by the organizations to which they give to reflect honesty, integrity, and genuine values.

A reputation of integrity is built with transparency and accountability. Most organizations are not required by law to disclose their financial statements unless they're in trouble or suspected of breaking the law. But fully disclosing financial records shows that you have nothing to hide and that all your practices are honorable, fair, and ethical. There are no gray areas hidden between the red numbers and the black ones.

We must maintain the same standards of integrity in all dimensions of our personal finances. If we can't afford something, we need to stick to our budget and not make a purchase until the money is saved up for it. If we owe taxes, we must pay them and not try to omit any facts about our income. If a salesclerk makes an error in our favor, we should tell them as soon as we realize it and return the money.

These kinds of choices show integrity. God is watching us, and he wants to bless us. Let's not stand in his way.

FAITHFUL STEWARDSHIP

The second value my dad taught me is stewardship. *Steward* is the Old English word for "manager." When we steward our finances, we manage them in a way that pleases God, who owns it all. We must develop responsibility and accountability in all of our practices, recognizing that how we spend our money is so much bigger than what we purchase, charge on our credit cards, or deposit in the bank. Everything we have comes from God—everything, down to each breath we take.

One of the most life-giving things we can do is get rid of an "owner mentality." When we hold tight to what we have, we fail to receive the gifts God wants to give us. We must be openhanded in our approach to all we're given—our possessions, our homes, our salaries, our cars, our property.

The goal of life is not to accumulate wealth and possessions. Our purpose in life is to handle God's resources as faithful managers, good stewards who look beyond the immediate personal effect of a decision and are guided instead by eternal principles.

> Whoever can be trusted with very little can also be trusted with much, and whoever is dishonest with very little will also be dishonest with much. So if you have not been trustworthy in handling worldly wealth, who will trust you with true riches? (Luke 16:10–11)

GENEROUS TO A FAULT

A third value I learned is generosity—living to give, as conduits of God's extravagant love and abundant provision. We are blessed to bless others. "Just as you excel in everything—in faith, in speech, in knowledge, in complete earnestness and in the love we have kindled in you—see that you also excel in this grace of giving" (2 Corinthians 8:7).

I challenge you to greater generosity. Give things away. Don't focus on how much you can make and spend or even save, but on how much you can give away. And remember, money isn't the only thing we can give. We can share our talents, hugs, smiles, and prayers.

God makes it clear in his Word how our attitude about giving impacts our lives (and since this is true, shouldn't we be looking to give away as much as we can?):

> Remember this: Whoever sows sparingly will also reap sparingly, and whoever sows generously will also reap generously. Each of you should give what you have decided in your heart to give, not reluctantly or under compulsion, for God loves a cheerful giver. (2 Corinthians 9:6–7).

Make no mistake—it's okay to have and enjoy possessions. I don't believe we must literally impoverish ourselves in order to prove our faith is genuine. Some people believe the only way to be holy is to sell everything, yet this can become just as misguided and all-consuming as acquiring everything.

It's all a matter of where our hearts are. When our focus is on acquiring, getting, earning, achieving, accumulating, and hoarding, we lose our spiritual focus on God. In Psalm 62:10, David makes this contrast clear and direct: "Do not trust in extortion or put vain hope in stolen goods; though your riches increase, do not set your heart on them."

We must remain anchored to God alone, not trusting in our

riches or setting our hearts on getting more. It's not wrong to have things; it's only wrong when things have us. So we rejoice in what God has given us, without demanding more or making that our goal.

If we make loving God and serving others our objective, there'll be no pain involved in giving away what we have. We'll have a deeper abiding joy that's not tied to what we own or anything money can buy. This is why I'm convinced that the best antidote when our hearts have drifted to the wrong place is generosity. Nothing breaks the spirit of materialism like generosity. We'll never go wrong if we keep remembering what our Master has made so clear: "You're far happier giving than getting" (Acts 20:35 MSG).

A generous heart gives more than money and possessions. You can spend time with someone just to enjoy his or her company, or phone someone to say you're thinking of and praying for them. Give your talents to serve others. Giving your attention and affection can be so simple, but it can make such a huge difference in another person's life. A timely hug can communicate far more than any material gift.

Here's a promise of fresh air from God's Word: "The generous will prosper; those who refresh others will themselves be refreshed" (Proverbs 11:25 NLT).

SEED MONEY

Finally, we must focus on the eternal impact we all can make with our resources. If we want to obey God and experience a breath of fresh air in our finances, we must focus on treasures in heaven.

Think about the return on your investments. Remember the parable of the talents? The master goes away and gives each of his servants a number of talents to invest. When he returns and inquires about what they've done with what he gave them, the first two servants tell him how they made wise investments and multiplied the returns. However, the third servant blew it. He buried his talents and did nothing with them whatsoever.

It's clear that God wants a return on all that he has given us:

> God is able to bless you abundantly, so that in all things at all times, having all that you need, you will abound in every good work. As it is written: "They have freely scattered their gifts to the poor; their righteousness endures forever." Now he who supplies seed to the sower and bread for food will also supply and increase your store of seed and will enlarge the harvest of your righteousness. You will be enriched in every way so that you can be generous on every occasion, and through us your generosity will result in thanksgiving to God. (2 Corinthians 9:8–11)

God gives talents to his people in order that his investments might grow. He gives seed to the sower in hopes of multiplying the harvest. He's looking for harvest-minded people who aren't going to hoard the seeds he gives them but will instead plant wisely and produce in abundance. This is the strategy of the Great Commission, the call placed on all who believe and trust Jesus with their lives to share this good news with everyone everywhere.

The bottom line of any accounts ledger should be on eternity—not short-term material profits. The purpose of money is to use it to grow the kingdom of God. Everything we do must be focused on the harvest. This is God's priority, and it should be ours as well:

> Do not store up for yourselves treasures on earth, where moths and vermin destroy, and where thieves break in and steal. But

> store up for yourselves treasures in heaven. . . . For where your treasure is, there your heart will be also. (Matthew 6:19–21)

FIRST THINGS FIRST

Now that we've looked at the four values—integrity, stewardship, generosity, and a focus on eternal impact—let's consider the practices that put these principles into action.

Let's begin with the practice of tithing. This is a simple practice, but one that trips up so many people.

The first portion of everything we receive—a *tithe*, as Scripture calls it—belongs to the Lord our God. People usually consider the tithe to be one-tenth of the whole of what we have, but I believe that the principle of tithing centers more on giving to God *first* rather than giving him a certain amount. The tithe is not just a percentage principle but a principle of firsts. It's an opportunity to declare who means the most to us and what we consider the most important priority in our lives. It's holy to the Lord, and he alone has the power to bless the rest of what we have.

Some people say that tithing is a "law principle," something that was instituted during the time of Moses and done away with after Christ's coming, but we need to realize that this practice shows up at least 2,500 years before the Levitical law was established. I see it first in the sacrifices offered by Cain and Abel, the sons of Adam and Eve. They each offered God something, and he was pleased with one offering but not the other. Why? What was the difference?

Let's look at the account and pay attention to the distinction between Cain's offering, which God did not find acceptable, and Abel's offering, which God accepted:

> Abel kept flocks, and Cain worked the soil. In the course of time Cain brought some of the fruits of the soil as an offering to the Lord. And Abel also brought an offering—fat portions from some of the firstborn of his flock. The Lord looked with favor on Abel and his offering, but on Cain and his offering he did not look with favor. (Genesis 4:2–5)

Abel brought the *firstborn* of his flock; Cain did not bring his firstfruits. God cannot accept an offering if it's not the first portion. We show our respect and appreciation to him by honoring him first.

As a boy, I learned from my dad what tithing meant. When I received money, whether an allowance or a ten-dollar bill inside a birthday card from grandparents, my father said, "Give the first to God, then think about the rest."

I'll be honest: I've always experienced unexplainable favor in my life with money and material possessions. I believe when we honor God first, he does indeed bless us, not as a quid pro quo transaction, but because he knows where our hearts are. He knows we're dedicated to advancing his kingdom with our resources. He doesn't want our stuff; God wants you and me. He wants to know where we place him on our list of priorities.

Tithing is a barometer of where our hearts are, a test to see if we're serious about trusting God and acknowledging him as the source of everything we have. We put God first by giving him the first of everything (not just money, but everything), because first things reveal where our treasure is. If we give him the first of our year, it says something to him. If we give him the first of our week, it speaks volumes. If we give him the first of our day, it's loud and clear. If we give him the first of our possessions, it shows we're serious about our commitment to him.

Although *tithe* literally means "tenth" or "tenth part," this percentage is used only as an equalizer so that we can participate equally and know we're giving God our first portions. We can't give equal amounts, but we can all give the first tenth of whatever we have. "A tithe of everything from the land, whether grain from the soil or fruit from the trees, belongs to the Lord; it is holy to the Lord" (Leviticus 27:30). It's possible to give 10 percent and not be tithing. That's because tithing is not giving one out of ten things; it's giving the first of the ten before using the other nine.

The whole point of tithing is to give to God *first*. "The purpose of tithing is to teach you always to put God first in your lives" (Deuteronomy 14:23 TLB). God obligates himself to bless first things and make them holy. He bestows first things with the power to bless the rest:

> In all your ways submit to him. . . . Honor the Lord with your wealth, with the firstfruits of all your crops; then your barns will be filled to overflowing, and your vats will brim over with new wine. (Proverbs 3:6–10)

THE SPACE BETWEEN

The second practice, margin, provides us with breathing room in our finances. Margin is simply the space between ourselves and our limits.[3] It allows room in between where we are now and where we will be in the future. Once again, it's a practice that looks beyond immediate gratification and convenience: "The wise store up choice food and olive oil, but fools gulp theirs down" (Proverbs 21:20).

Margin enables us to say yes to unexpected opportunities that

God places before us, while giving us the freedom to say no to opportunities that don't fit his plans for our lives. It helps us endure lean times with confidence.

Margin works in every area. If we plan to show up fifteen minutes earlier than each meeting or appointment, we'll arrive calm and prepared, not rushed and stressed. We'll have more peace in our lives. We won't have to drive faster because we're running late. We can relax throughout the day knowing that margin protects us from any upcoming storms.

We've used the principle of margin in our home. You can imagine how hectic a morning can be with five kids getting ready for school. So we've encouraged everyone to be ready to walk out the door fifteen minutes before time to leave. When everyone's ready, we hang out in the kitchen, discussing the day ahead, planning beyond it. Everyone's relaxed, and we begin the day with peace.

If we apply margin to our finances, we can experience amazing peace in that area as well. If we set some money aside for emergencies, we won't freak out when the car breaks down or the roof leaks. If we have a plan for the long run, we can relax in the short term. Margin reflects good stewardship.

THE MYTH OF MORE

Speaking of a plan for the long run, finding the discipline to follow a budget is our third practice. We must set ceilings on our expenditures, then stick to them. Having a budget gives us a compass to help us navigate each day's expenses and opportunities. When we stay on budget, we remain on course for where we want to be: unstressed, responsible, peace-filled, and secure. Budgetary discipline provides ongoing reassurance that we're living for God and not for things.

Most people see budgets as restrictive; I've found the opposite to be true, even with our church's budget. Our Church of the Highlands budget never exceeds 90 percent of the previous year's income. Since our giving increases each year, that margin takes off considerable pressure, while also enabling us to say yes to a lot of proposals. Our staff knows we have resources to fund worthy initiatives, which brings a lot of life and fresh air to what they're seeking to do for the kingdom.

The Bible's focus on budgets goes back over three thousand years. You'll remember King Solomon, one of the richest and wisest men who ever lived. As described in Ecclesiastes, he denied himself no pleasure, yet found himself miserable. Basically he discovered that things can never satisfy the heart.

We're back to the law of diminishing returns: The more we have, the less it satisfies us. You see this every year at Christmastime. Everyone wants to make this holiday bigger, better, and more special than last year's. With all the pressure from advertisers with sales and special promotions, it's no wonder we think we must spend more to make it better. The problem is, many people still have not paid for last year's holiday!

One of Solomon's wise observations resonates today more than ever: "Those who love money will never have enough" (Ecclesiastes 5:10 NLT). We see this in families, businesses, even churches—everyone wants more than they have. Why has our nation's debt tripled and quadrupled in recent years? The more we spend, the more we want to spend.

The myth of more would have us believe that more stuff will satisfy us, even after we've already experienced numerous disappointments. I remember calling and canceling a magazine subscription—only to have a telemarketer phone me an hour later with an offer to resubscribe! Did they really think I'd changed my mind in just an hour? Solomon wrote, "The more you have, the more people come to help you spend it" (Ecclesiastes 5:11 NLT).

The great irony of wealth is that it can make our lives seem easier or more pleasurable, but it can't bring us peace, joy, or a genuine love for other people. Oh, it might buy us some "friends" for a while. But money can't improve our marriages or heal a sick child. It can't provide us with the intimacy of loving another person.

In fact, having more money and possessions can actually rob us of whatever peace we might have had. That's because when we own more stuff, we have more stuff to worry about. We have to worry about maintenance and upkeep, repairs and emergencies, theft and accidents. We have to spend money on all those worries as well, either through insurance or services to maintain the beloved possession. While we'd think that people with more money would have less stress, the opposite is generally true: "The rich seldom get a good night's sleep" (Ecclesiastes 5:12 NLT).

The solution is to live by principle, within your means, and following a plan that reflects your priorities and values. Don't buy into the myth of more—literally! Don't buy into the world's other practices either.

I've seen big problems develop in churches when they adopt certain practices from the world of corporate culture. Building campaigns, fundraisers, faith promises—we don't do them at our church. Honestly, I think most people hate them—the pressure, the obligation, the unspoken messages sent by such endeavors. I think if you stick with God's plan for raising money, you have nothing to worry about. So we don't ask people for money. We ask God for what we need and trust him to convey the need to his people.

THE PRINCIPLE OF PEACE

Finally, let me point out an interesting insight I first heard from my friend Pastor Craig Groeschel. "Prince" is the root of the word *principles*. The implication is that principles were originally royal decrees that all the subjects of the land had to obey.

One of the names given to Jesus is "Prince of Peace." You may recall it from a familiar verse that's read at Christmastime: "For to us a child is born, to us a son is given, and the government will be on his shoulders. And he will be called Wonderful Counselor, Mighty God, Everlasting Father, Prince of Peace" (Isaiah 9:6). The Hebrew phrase for "Prince of Peace" is *sar shalom*. In Hebrew, *sar* means the one in charge, the lord of the land, the chief, the general. It's not just royalty, like Prince Charming; it's much more authoritative. It's where we get the title *czar* for Russian emperors and the title *caesar* for emperors of Rome.

Shalom may be a more familiar word. It means rest, tranquility, wholeness, completeness, contentment. So together, the two words *sar shalom* can also be translated accurately as "Captain of Completeness" or "General of Tranquility" or "Chief of Wholeness" or even "Lord of Contentment." And if Jesus is all these things—if he is indeed the Lord of Peace—we must realize that there is no peace if he is not our Lord.

These two words—*peace* and *Lord*—and their impact on our lives are fundamental to having fresh air in all areas of our existence. I'm always amazed that some people think they can do whatever they please and then wonder why they don't have peace in their lives. They make immoral decisions, then pray to have peace. They yell at their spouse and kids, then wonder why there's no peace at home. They max out all their credit cards and never tithe, then wonder how they can have financial peace as described in the Bible.

So much of our stress in life comes from not following Jesus's principles, which were given for our own well-being. The solution is simple but not easy. We must get under his lordship and make him the Prince of Peace in our lives.

When it comes to money, following his principles brings peace. These aren't just good ideas or solid business models. They're not just wise sayings or clever rules. They are principles, royal decrees, from the King of kings and the Prince of Peace. God wants to bless us, not so we can live worry-free in luxury and affluence, but so we experience something far more precious: his peace, his joy, his contentment. What he gives is indeed priceless!

BREATHING LESSON

A breath of fresh air in finances begins with values—principles. When you have solid biblical principles, you can live by principle instead of pressure.

After you settle in on the guiding principles, begin to work on the practices. You may have to start slow, but start now and you'll immediately begin to sense the wind filling your sails. Change one thing today about how you relate to your money—giving to someone in need, giving God what is his, or choosing not to purchase something you don't really need.

If budgets and big-picture strategies seem overwhelming right now, pray and ask God to show you just one thing to change about how you handle your finances.

Remember this—a farmer who plants only a few seeds will get a small crop. But the one who plants generously will get a generous crop. You must each decide in your heart how much to give. And don't give reluctantly or in response to pressure. "For God loves a person who gives cheerfully." And God will generously provide all you need. Then you will always have everything you need and plenty left over to share with others.

—2 Corinthians 9:6–8 NLT

11

ROOM TO REST

A field that has rested gives a bountiful crop.

OVID

I recall taking my first sabbatical, an extended break of eight weeks intended to provide rest to my body, mind, and soul. For years, my friends in ministry as well as my mentors (especially those older than me) had advised me to take one—not just a mini version or one in name only, but a genuine Sabbath season that would give me room to rest, away from all my usual responsibilities and commitments. Honestly, I didn't think I needed one. I'd always enjoyed ministry—in fact, it energizes me. I'd always believed in that saying, "If you love what you do, you'll never work a day in your life."

Besides, I had regularly taken a weekly Sabbath day off and was consistent about actually making it a day of rest. Since Sunday was my hardest workday—I preached as many as five times—I would usually take Monday as my day off. I joked that if Lionel Richie had been a pastor, he'd have changed his hit song "Easy Like Sunday Morning" to "Easy Like Monday Morning."

I love my days off. I grab a cup of coffee and my Bible and spend time with God in prayer and worship. Then I usually watch some online church services from a list of my ministry friends around the nation. I open my Bible and take notes, just as if I were a member of their congregation. I always tell people, "I go to church on Mondays." It's been a great routine that really feeds me.

But 2011 was different. After the death of my father in 2010 and my father-in-law in early 2011, and after twenty-eight years of ministry and ten years of "pedal-to-the-metal" church planting, I was deep-down tired, emotionally exhausted—the kind of tired you don't realize is there because you've grown so used to it, pressing through it day after day.

Our church leadership team saw it in me. Our overseers, our trustees, and our elders all agreed it was time for me to take an extended break—an eight-week sabbatical.

At first I was hesitant. I'd never been out of the pulpit for more than two consecutive weekends. Would the church be okay without me for that long? Or a deeper, scarier question: Would I be okay without my role at the church for that long? What would I do for eight weeks? But the more I thought about it, the more I knew I needed it.

REST LIKE YOU MEAN IT

My sabbatical was wonderful—life-changing and life-giving. I never read an email, I never answered a phone call, and my golf game improved—well, at least a little. During the eight weeks, I spent four weeks at home, two weeks with my wife in Italy celebrating our twenty-fifth wedding anniversary, and two weeks on the Gulf Coast with Tammy and our kids. It couldn't have been a better experience, or come at a better time.

I learned many things—about myself, about God, about my family, and about how to experience God's refreshment in our lives. Here are the three biggest discoveries.

First, it took three weeks before I completely disconnected from my work responsibilities and went an entire day without wondering how things were going at the church without me. I had thought I was good at separating myself from work when I wasn't there, but the truth is that I thought about it most of the time.

Second, I learned that I'd lost my ability to recognize when I was tired. I'd figured out how to run on adrenaline and push through it. I needed to listen to my body and recognize and respect my need for true rest.

Finally, I realized that I needed to make a deliberate commitment to rest—daily, weekly, monthly, and annually. I needed a comprehensive life routine that included rest as a key component. Since my sabbatical, my routine includes the crucial rest time my mind, body, and soul require in order to remain healthy, balanced, and in touch with God's leading.[1]

NOTHING DOING

The truth is that all of us are probably more tired than we realize or want to admit. This deep fatigue may be robbing us of joy and siphoning off our energy. We've never stopped to rest and recalibrate.

Think honestly about your life right now. Do you ever get tired just thinking of all you've got to do today, this week, this month? Do you feel just as tired on Monday morning as you do on Friday afternoon? You may feel not only physically fatigued, but out of emotional, mental, and spiritual energy as well. Those feelings are telling you something.

Personal indicators like these are there to remind us to rest. We need balance in our lives or we lose our sense of direction and run the risk of breakdown. If we don't take rest seriously, we'll be forced to learn its vital significance the hard way. We can't function without true rest; it's simply the way we're made. So often we look for ways to relax or unwind that aren't healthy, and we find ourselves developing bad habits that ultimately make us even more exhausted. Jesus warned about a hurried lifestyle, the kind many of us live today: "Be careful, or your hearts will be weighed down with carousing, drunkenness and the anxieties of life, and that day will close on you suddenly like a trap" (Luke 21:34). He wants us to be on guard against getting stretched to the limit.

When our bodies and emotions are pulled every which way and stretched to the breaking point, the risk of making sinful choices climbs off the charts. We no longer think straight or with a long-term perspective. We have less clarity about our priorities and what we're really committed to in our lives.

If you want to experience a breath of fresh air in your life, you have to resist the temptation to keep going at the same pace all the time. In fact, I have three warnings for you to help you pay attention and realize your own need for rest.

First, beware of overestimating your ability to endure a heavy load or hectic pace. Your personal pride may shame you into pushing through when you really need to rest. Workaholics have such a deep-seated sense of pride that they no longer even hear their body's cries for rest. You and I are not superheroes. We're not God. We're human. And we need rest.

Sometimes we give our bosses and family members too much power over what we do, allowing them to push us beyond healthy limits. If we're constantly on call, either at work or as a caregiver for an ill family member, we may need to be honest with others about what we can actually handle.

Next, beware of out-of-control schedules that do not include a firm margin for rest. (Remember that *margin* simply means space between ourselves and our limits, something held in reserve for unanticipated situations.) Very few people say they have plenty of time to do the things they need and want to do. Instead they feel pulled and pushed, obligated and committed, forced by habit into fulfilling the urgent agendas of everyone around them. Most of the activities on our schedules do not contribute to the vision or goals we've set for our lives. Yet we keep doing them. Over and over again, we stay on the merry-go-round of constant busyness, one thing after another. But no rest.

My third warning is to beware of substitute solutions. Most people know they need rest in their lives, but they try to fix the problem with a short-term solution rather than the one God gave us. They think, *Well, I'll take a half day off* when they know it will be consumed by playing catch-up on all the other things demanding their time and attention. They think, *I'll just take a sleeping pill* or *I'll just have a drink to relax.* Instead of taking time away for real body and soul rest, they rely on a placebo, a substitute. The problem is, there is no substitute for true rest.

IT'S THE PRINCIPLE THAT COUNTS

God's Word is clear: Honoring the Sabbath is a major way he designed for us to be refreshed. And please realize that the Sabbath is a principle—it's not a law requiring us to honor the seventh day, but a truth about how we're made and what we really need. "It will be a sign between me and the Israelites forever, for in six days the Lord made the heavens and the earth, and on the seventh day he rested and was *refreshed*" (Exodus 31:17).

All of God's laws were designed with our well-being in mind. The motivation behind a law is what we should be focused on, not the external logistics of how it's exercised. If we're doing anything just because God said to do it, our obedience can easily become legalistic. We end up going through the motions just like the Pharisees, the religious leaders of Jesus's day who acted certain ways so that they could be smugly self-righteous. In their hearts, they clearly were not focused on loving God but on manipulating God's principles for their own agendas.

God provides principles in his Word to give us abundant life. When we obey those principles—not just the semantics of the law—his rules become life-giving truth. So God gave us the Sabbath for our own good. Jesus certainly made it clear that keeping the Sabbath was never intended to be a rule but a way of life: "The Sabbath was made for man, not man for the Sabbath" (Mark 2:27).

To understand this day of rest, we need to understand the origin of the word and the concept behind it. The word *Sabbath* was derived from the Hebrew word *shabbat*, which comes from the Hebrew verb *shavat*. Both words refer to a stop in the normal routine, to actively and deliberately cease function. It's a concept, not a day on the calendar. The idea means taking one day out of seven to stop doing what we've been doing and focus on restoration, relaxation, and renewal.

So the idea of Sabbath is to stop working for wages and competing for rewards. Stop running and going and striving and doing, and just *be*.

When was the last time you weren't worried about what time it was? When was the last time you weren't on the clock? Maybe for some of us, a real way to honor and enjoy the Sabbath would be to go a whole day each week without looking at our watches.

Sabbath is about playing and relaxing. Reading and studying spiritual material—not because you have to but because you want to. Taking leisurely strolls outdoors and enjoying the beauty of God's creation. Talking with friends and enjoying the company of your family. Attending church services and worshiping with others. Praying and meditating. Spending time with God without feeling obligated or rushed. Just hanging out together.

While part of your Sabbath may be spent alone, it wasn't necessarily intended to be experienced alone. Sabbath is not just personal but communal. It's about helping one another remember to relax and rest, to enjoy one another without a formal purpose, agenda, or production-minded motive.

At the heart of it, Sabbath is a day to celebrate our freedom from human rules and regulations and to remember our real purpose: to love God and to serve his kingdom.

Why is this so vital to our well-being? As we work and do all week long, we easily develop an inflated, self-centered idea of our own power and self-sufficiency. The Sabbath is a constant reminder that for one day a week, we are dispensable to work and to the world—but not to our families, our community, or God.

Like the tithe, the Sabbath principle demonstrates that by

honoring God's design, we get more done with less. We can get more out of 90 percent of our income when we tithe than from 100 percent when we don't. We get more out of six days of work and responsibilities than if we stay on duty all seven days.

The first mention of the Sabbath in Scripture raises interesting theological questions:

> By the seventh day God had finished the work he had been doing; so on the seventh day he rested from all his work. Then God blessed the seventh day and made it holy, because on it he rested from all the work of creating that he had done. (Genesis 2:2–3)

First, why does an all-powerful God need to rest? If he's omnipotent, how could he be tired and need to take a day off?

This passage translated literally means, "He was refreshed." And, along with the fact that we don't see God taking a day of rest anywhere else in Scripture, that leads me to believe that God clearly did not need this for himself but did it to set an example for us.

It's important to note as well that the Sabbath day actually comes first and not last. Although it shows up last in the creation account, God establishes it for us as something to be done first. When I visited Israel, I was surprised to learn that the Jewish people mark the start of each new day at sundown. In other words, they begin their day with rest! As someone there told me, "If you rest well, you'll never get tired."

So often we rest only when we're extremely tired or past our limits, but God wants us to make rest a regular priority so we avoid exhaustion. We're supposed to take a Sabbath first thing in our week, so we're rested and equipped to be as productive and focused as possible.

WORK TO REST

It takes a lot of work to rest in our world today. That sounds a bit contradictory, but we must make every effort to get the real rest our bodies, minds, and souls need. We must be vigilant and deliberate to ensure that we get what God established as essential to our ongoing welfare. "Let us, therefore, make every effort to enter that rest, so that no one will perish by following their example of disobedience" (Hebrews 4:11).

Many of us need to relearn how to slow down and come to a complete soul standstill. We must reorder our lives and start being intentional about taking care of ourselves in godly, life-giving ways. Resting is not being lazy or shirking our duties. Again, the irony is that we're actually much more productive when we regularly include rest in our schedules than when we keep pushing ourselves and trying to do it all.

Incorporating Sabbath as an active part of your life will require you to set firm boundaries and honor them. You must be intentional about it. You should include holy days in your schedule and even holy moments throughout your day. (The word *holy* simply means "set apart," and that's what I mean here.) If you don't deliberately designate certain times to rest and spend with God and your family, you're unlikely to do it. More "urgent" matters will always demand your attention if you let them.

Maybe a regular date night with your spouse is part of what it means for you to keep the Sabbath. Or it could be a regular time with God each day, as well as a special time once a week or once a month. Maybe you need to plan fun family celebrations a way to honor the Sabbath as well. It's so easy to give our families what's left over in our lives instead of the primary attention they deserve.

In a basic way, including Sabbath in your life may mean looking at your priorities and revising your usual schedule and routines. Maybe you need more margin in your life so that you're not always running late, stressed to the max, and trying to cram in one more thing each day. Maybe it's time to give your most important activities the best part of your day. Maybe it's time to put the important things first. "In vain you rise early and stay up late, toiling for food to eat—for he grants sleep to those he loves" (Psalm 127:2).

We simply must not ignore God's call to rest. In the Bible, we see an entire generation who didn't enter the Promised Land simply because they had not learned to honor and practice God's ways:

> That is why the Holy Spirit says, "Today when you hear his voice, don't harden your hearts as Israel did when they rebelled, when they tested me in the wilderness. There your ancestors tested and tried my patience, even though they saw my miracles for forty years. So I was angry with them, and I said, 'Their hearts always turn away from me. They refuse to do what I tell them.' So in my anger I took an oath: 'They will never enter my place of rest.'" (Hebrews 3:7–11 NLT)

Clearly, the people of Israel wouldn't listen to the warning signs. They did their own thing and ignored what God had established for their own benefit.

I think God gives us the same warning today, but most of us are not listening. Yet if we ignore God's call for rest, we're going to get to the end of our lives and regret our hurried lifestyle. Worse, we are likely to realize we have little of eternal value to show for it.

If we're not careful, our bodies will force us to come to a grinding halt. Our mortal bodies have limitations and need to be honored and respected and appreciated as the temples in which God's Spirit lives. But so often we just keep pushing and pushing. We rush from thing to thing, crisis to crisis, urgent deadline to urgent deadline, without realizing the toll it's taking on us.

A pastor friend of mine told me about a tour he took to Israel. While outside Jerusalem, he saw a flock of sheep, but no one was leading it. Then he saw someone behind the flock that assumed was the shepherd. Still, that contradicted everything he knew from the Bible about shepherds leading the flock and the sheep following the shepherd's voice. So my friend asked his tour guide why that particular shepherd was following the flock instead of leading it, and the guide said, "Oh, that's not the shepherd. That's the butcher!"

Our shepherd leads us; butchers drive us to our own destruction. In Psalm 23, we're told that the Lord is our shepherd and that he leads us beside still, quiet waters. He restores our soul and breathes fresh air into our lives. He wants us calm and peaceful, joyful and rested—not panicked and running from the butcher behind us.

REST STOP

Rest also requires our faith. Real rest doesn't come from a day off or even from taking a vacation or sabbatical. It comes when our souls are connected to God's power. It comes when our minds relax because we know God is in charge. It comes when we're not stressed since we're trusting God to guide and lead us. Rest comes from our genuine reliance on God to meet all our needs each day. "We see that because of their unbelief they were not able to enter his rest" (Hebrews 3:19 NLT).

As people of faith, we're not bound by the dimensions of this world. A day of rest allows us to get a heavenly perspective, to get away from the natural and into the supernatural. When we have faith, we can remain calm and contented. But when we don't have faith, we worry and fret and get anxious over every little thing.

TAKE MY YOKE

It takes faith to obey and to do what we don't fully understand or want to do—including to rest. And even though we have to work at it, finding rest is not hard because the real secret to rest is to get close to Jesus.

Jesus knew what it was like to need rest and to set time aside so he could be renewed and refreshed, both by spending time with his disciples and time alone with his Father. He often urged his disciples to get away from the crowds with him. He knew they needed to come apart before they came apart. "Because so many people were coming and going that they did not even have a chance to eat, he said to them, 'Come with me by yourselves to a quiet place and get some rest'" (Mark 6:31).

Daily pressure took a toll on Jesus's disciples, as it does for us. Fortunately, his offer is the same today as well:

> Come to me, all of you who are weary and carry heavy burdens, and I will give you rest. Take my yoke upon you. Let me teach you, because I am humble and gentle at heart, and you will find rest for your souls. For my yoke is easy to bear, and the burden I give you is light. (Matthew 11:28–30 NLT).

Jesus doesn't want us to stop producing. In fact, he encourages us to find true rest by taking on another yoke—his yoke. As an attachment to the harness on oxen or donkeys, a wooden yoke kept the animals plowing down the same row in the right direction. Once again, it seems odd or contradictory to think that we rest by taking on a yoke, something designed to force an animal to work. But notice that Jesus says: "Take *my* yoke" (Matthew 11:29)—in other words, we've got the wrong one on. There's a way to be purposeful in our work without growing weary and exhausted. We simply have to go to him and carry only what he gives us to carry—and nothing more.

In order to experience the refreshment that comes from practicing the principle of Sabbath rest, I recommend four strategies.

First, stop at regular intervals even if you don't feel tired or think you need the rest. Some people claim that they "work hard and play hard," which is great, but playing hard is not the same thing as Sabbath rest. Part of our rest must involve becoming still before God and acknowledging our reliance on him. "Be still, and know that I am God" (Psalm 46:10).

Second, remove external distractions and interruptions. We're so overstimulated in our world today. A friend and I were having coffee, and during our conversation he kept checking email and texting on his smartphone. Finally I said, "I thought this was your day off." He looked at me sheepishly and said, "Well, it is. This is a much slower pace for me than usual."

With our constant bombardment from media and technology, it's no wonder we suffer from societal ADD. Real rest requires times of silence, a fast from the normal ways we communicate with the world. I encourage you to take one day a week to unplug—no email, no texts, no phone calls except for emergencies. Let your body and mind rest from the constant influx of information.

Third, I recommend a deliberate plan for embracing your

community of family and friends and engaging them in a time of worshiping God together. It doesn't have to be a formal church service or Bible study. It can simply be gathering around the old piano and singing some worship songs together. It can be a time of discussing what you're thankful for that day around the dinner table. It can be a weekly time where you share prayer requests and praises with a group of friends. Coming together as a family and a community and worshiping God restores us more than we realize. We get a bigger picture than just our own lives and can focus on what God is doing in the lives of others we care about.

Finally, I encourage you to learn the art of celebration. "Feasting" is what it's often called in the Bible—times when all the stops are pulled out and you gather everyone together to celebrate a special occasion, a rare event, an amazing achievement, or simply the fact that you're all together in one place. Special activities feed the soul and allow us to step outside the challenges and responsibilities of everyday life.

Certainly, Christmas and Easter afford us wonderful opportunities to celebrate and feast together, but we must do this more than twice a year. These don't need to be elaborate affairs, either—just times to acknowledge the beautiful and good in our lives.

The reality is that rest is essential. God knew this when he made us and demonstrated its value to us so that we would grasp just how important it is. Going at full tilt is the way of the world. Striving, working, hustling, and hurrying are supposedly required if we want to get ahead in life. But God tells us that if we want to experience real momentum and life-giving breath in our lives, we must practice the principle of the Sabbath. "My Presence will go with you, and I will give you rest" (Exodus 33:14).

We must do everything we can to do nothing. God has promised us that when we do, we'll be refreshed.

BREATHING LESSON

Chances are, you really needed to hear the message in this chapter. I hope it's been life-giving and refreshing, but I want to challenge you to do more than just think about what you want to do differently. I challenge you to do something about it *today*. I truly believe that this principle is God's remedy for burnout.

So take the first step right now. If nothing else, stop where you are and close your eyes and just breathe for sixty seconds. If you can do it for five whole minutes, all the better.

Next, look at your calendar or appointment app or wherever you keep your schedule. What needs to change in order for you to incorporate and practice Sabbath in your life?

I encourage you to set aside time every morning—even for just ten minutes—to refocus your spirit on God, your soul on his Word, and your life on the things that really matter.

Finally, I challenge you to unplug one whole day this coming week. Use this time to be with your family doing something you love—enjoying a great meal together, going for a walk, playing a board game. I think you'll discover that times of rest and reflection are often the most productive moments of your week.

> Teach us to number our days and recognize how few they are; help us to spend them as we should.
>
> —Psalm 90:12 TLB

PART THREE

FINDING THE SOURCE OF BREATH

12

THE SOURCE OF BREATH

The answer, my friend, is blowin' in the wind,
the answer is blowin' in the wind.

BOB DYLAN

By now, I hope you're convinced that a life totally refreshed with wind in your sails is more than possible. But I realize you may be a little frustrated too. Perhaps you're beginning to understand the rush-of-grace, breath-of-fresh-air concept and its application—but you're still not sure how to live it out every day. To some degree, you can learn to live a better life by trying harder, being more focused and organized, and developing healthier habits. However, these changes provide only limited results.

The greatest discovery I made while going through the doldrums was that my root problem was spiritual, even though my struggles appeared to be physical and circumstantial. We often forget that here on earth we are spiritual beings (having a mind, will, and emotions) living in a body. We are not physical beings having temporary spiritual experiences; we're spiritual beings having temporary physical experiences.

I'm convinced that in everything we face, we must deal with it first spiritually. I'm not saying we should neglect physical checkups, medical treatment, and visits to doctors and counselors. I believe in using all the practical resources God provides for us to heal and to find refreshment and restoration. But if we recognize that we're spiritual beings and address our problems first from this perspective, we may discover a lifelong solution.

In my case, I drifted from purposefulness and intimate connection with God—and ended up in a pit of despair. I needed more than encouraging words and new habits. I needed a transformed life.

You and I don't have to settle for a mediocre life or try harder to be a "good Christian." God has provided us with a continual power source, best friend, trail guide, and direct link to him. He never intended for us to make life work through our own efforts. He has always wanted to be intimately involved with our lives. This is the very reason he sent his Son to earth to live as a man and defeat death once and for all. With this victory, Jesus gave us a gift, an ongoing breath of fresh air in our lives.

Are you ready for this book's "big reveal"? It may or may not surprise you. The source of the blast of life-breath in us is the Holy Spirit of God. You may have heard or read explanations of the Holy Spirit in your life, and I hope they were helpful. Most of the time, however, I think we misunderstand this gift from God. In these final chapters, I invite you to rethink what you've been taught or just assumed about the Spirit. My hope is that you'll gain a more accurate understanding and a more intimate experience of his presence in your life.

BREATH OF HEAVEN

The word *spirit* is mentioned more than eight hundred times in our English translations of Scripture. In the Old Testament, the Hebrew word is *ruwach*, which literally means "a violent exhalation, a blast of breath, a strong wind." We find it used in the second verse of the Bible: "Now the earth was formless and empty, darkness was over the surface of the deep, and the Spirit [*ruwach*] of God was hovering over the waters" (Genesis 1:2).

Imagine this dark, murky body of water with God's breath hovering over it, perhaps stirring up the surface with its force. His breath seems to be the very energy force from which he created everything—earth, heavens, oceans, land, animals, fish, birds, sun, moon, stars, and of course, the first man and first woman, Adam and Eve. It's pretty amazing to think that every created thing began with the breath of God.

In the New Testament, the Greek word for this same kind of breath is *pneuma*, which also conveys a breath or wind, a current of air, a strong breeze. It too is usually translated as "spirit," referring to the Holy Spirit, who comes alongside us and empowers us with God's presence. As Jesus said, "The Spirit [*pneuma*—breath] gives life; the flesh counts for nothing. The words I have spoken to you—they are full of the Spirit [*pneuma*—breath] and life" (John 6:63).

Both *ruwach* and *pneuma* carry a sense of force, an active, living energy that blows in and brings life. This is exactly what the Holy Spirit came to do—breathe new life into us. God doesn't care about our "religious experiences" as much as he cares about giving us an abundance of spiritual fresh air. Too often, we reduce our faith to a stagnant exercise that we try to do perfectly, yet we never feel we have the necessary ability, energy, or power. We're trying to sail out of the doldrums but don't know where to find the wind.

AS THE WIND BLOWS

If the best way to describe the Holy Spirit is as *breath* or *wind*, let's consider the implications. Most of us feel more comfortable with things we can see and touch than things we sense or feel on the inside. Many people are uncomfortable with the notion of the Holy Spirit because they want something or someone they can relate to face-to-face. While this is understandable, we must remember that it takes faith to be in relationship with God.

To receive God's breath of life, we must live by faith and live faithfully. That means being comfortable with the unknown, the unseen, the things we don't understand. But that doesn't mean the Spirit should remain some vague, mysterious, abstract aspect of God that's beyond our understanding. If we think through the characteristics of wind, we can gain a clearer idea of the Spirit and his role in our lives.

Wind is unseen. Wind is something we feel and experience but don't see. We can observe its effects and its impact on leaves and trees, kites and windmills, but we never actually see the wind itself. But that doesn't keep us from acknowledging its reality.

Similarly, we must realize that while the Spirit can't be seen, he can be felt, experienced, and observed in action. When our church was still meeting at a high school, I remember standing at the door after one particular Sunday morning service, shaking hands and talking with people as they left. When I asked one particular first-time visitor if he'd enjoyed the service, he got a funny look on his face. "Preacher," he said, "there was something in that room today. Something different."

He didn't know what it was—he couldn't see it—but it drew him back the next week. Simply put, it was the presence of God.

The Spirit is undeniable, real, and refreshing. We may get frustrated because we can't quantify and objectify the Spirit; we must instead rely on faith. And the Bible defines faith this way: "Faith is confidence in what we hope for and assurance about what we do not see" (Hebrews 11:1).

After Jesus was resurrected, his disciple named Thomas heard from his friends that Jesus was alive again. But he said to them, 'Unless I see the nail marks in his hands and put my finger where the nails were, and put my hand into his side, I will not believe'" (John 20:25). Jesus soon gave this disciple what he asked for:

> He said to Thomas, "Put your finger here; see my hands. Reach out your hand and put it into my side. Stop doubting and believe." Thomas said to him, "My Lord and my God!" Then Jesus told him, "Because you have seen me, you have believed; blessed are those who have not seen and yet have believed." (John 20:27–29)

The Spirit requires us to put doubts aside and trust our Father. We can feel the Spirit without seeing him, like the wind. We can know he's there.

Wind is unpredictable. From the cool summer breeze that caresses us on a front porch swing to the furious tornado whipping at a hundred miles per hour, we know that wind changes speed and direction frequently. It goes where it wants.

The Holy Spirit moves unpredictably as well. Jesus told the Pharisee Nicodemus, "The wind [*pneuma*] blows wherever it pleases. You hear its sound, but you cannot tell where it comes from or where it is going. So it is with everyone born of the Spirit" (John 3:8). Jesus made it explicitly clear that the Holy Spirit moves in a seemingly unknowable way.

This can make a lot of us uncomfortable. Most people like everything orderly and in its place. Yet the Spirit-Wind can blow through and quickly change that order.

Why is this a key part of the Spirit's essence? I believe it's because if the Spirit was predictable, we'd put our trust in a system—the structure, the kind of cause-and-effect behavior that leads to legalism rather than relationship. If we could consistently predict the Spirit's movement, we'd focus on how to accomplish things without him.

God wants us to depend on him and interact with him on a continual basis, daily, hourly. But because of our selfish inclination toward personal comfort and convenience, we'd rather not deal with constant change and uncertainty.

Have you ever wondered why Jesus used different methods or techniques to heal people? On one occasion (seen in Mark 8:22–26), people brought forward a blind man and asked Jesus to touch and heal him. Instead, Christ spit on the man's eyes. If I'd been the guy who brought my blind friend to be healed, I'd be getting nervous. *Spit? Really?* It's almost as if Jesus was saying, "Just so you know the power is not in the method, I'll heal him in a creative, unexpected way." Obviously, Jesus could have instantly willed it, and the man would've been healed (as he did for the blind beggar Bartimaeus, in Mark 10:46–52). But there's a clear sense that Jesus, knowing our human nature, wants our focus to be on him, not on the how.

God's ways are not your ways. His thoughts are not your thoughts. To receive all he has for you, you have to get comfortable with the unexpected. You have to rely on him instead of what your mental assumptions tell you. You have to accept mystery as part of the relationship.

Wind is powerful. Wind can generate electricity, sail a ship, or destroy an entire city. Wind has power. And the Holy Spirit, the breath of God, is about power—supernatural power. This kind of divine, unseen, unpredictable power has been part of our faith from the time of Pentecost.

In nineteenth-century America, revivalist Charles Finney described his first encounter with God's Spirit as being "like a wave of electricity, going through and through me. Indeed it seemed to come in waves and waves of liquid love; for I could not express it in any other way. It seemed like the very breath of God."[1]

I'm sure all of us want that kind of power in our lives, though we may think it's easier to serve God on a merely intellectual level. If we can contain something in our thoughts and analyze it, we feel we have at least some control over it. Even Jesus's disciples were preoccupied with knowledge *about* God rather than a direct relationship with him, as when they asked Jesus (in Acts 1:5-8) about specific dates for the final coming of his kingdom. Jesus told them that this was not for them to know. Instead he emphasized that they should focus on experiencing the Spirit's coming. Most of us don't need more information; we need power. We don't need inspiring words about God; we need the inspired presence of God's Spirit breathing life into us.

An intellectual gospel is always in danger of creating a God who looks like us, one who's our size. If we've got to understand God before we can experience him, God can be no bigger than our own brains. We need more than human effort and ability; we need the breath wind of God to blow. "'Not by might nor by power, but by my Spirit [breath of fresh air]', says the LORD Almighty" (Zechariah 4:6).

The apostle Paul depended on the Holy Spirit. He wrote, "Our gospel came to you not simply with words but also with power, with the Holy Spirit [breath of fresh air] and deep conviction" (1 Thessalonians 1:5). His prayer for the Christians at Ephesus is my prayer for you: "Be filled with the Spirit [breath of fresh air]" (Ephesians 5:18). My hope is that you will begin getting acquainted with God's Spirit in a new and refreshing way. May you be filled with his life-giving breath and forever changed.

BREATHING LESSON

When and where did you first learn about the Holy Spirit? How did this shape your relationship with God, both positively and negatively? How would you describe your current relationship with the Holy Spirit?

I encourage you to sort through your ideas and feelings connected to the Holy Spirit and examine which ones come from God's Word, which ones come from your direct experience with him, and which ones come from hearsay and what others have told you or taught you. My hope is that you will make room in your heart for everything he wants to offer you.

> The Spirit of God, who raised Jesus from the dead, lives in you. And just as God raised Christ Jesus from the dead, he will give life to your mortal bodies by this same Spirit living within you.
>
> —Romans 8:11 NLT

13

A FRIEND LIKE NO OTHER

The intimate friendship of the
Holy Spirit be with all of you.

2 CORINTHIANS 13:14 MSG

I remember the first time I heard about it. I was probably twelve years old, and our church was having a business meeting to discuss it. I really wasn't clear what *it* was, but it was causing a stir. Years later, I discovered that our church was fighting about (uh, I mean discussing) a doctrinal issue concerning the "Holy Ghost." At the time, it was all very confusing because lots of people were saying we had to stay away from other people who had "received the Holy Ghost." Okay, sounds good to me. I mean, who wants to be around people who are hanging around with ghosts, right?

From that moment on, whenever I heard about people who were gullible enough to believe in the Holy Ghost, or who "spoke in tongues," I was wary. I thought they must be in some kind of hypnotic trance. That wasn't our kind of faith; that kind of thing was for the tambourine-and-hair-in-a-bun crowd. Stay away!

As the years went on, I learned to dismantle my misconceptions and my inherited prejudices about the Holy Spirit. One of the main reasons was that my own Christian experience ended up being a failure, to say the least. As I shared earlier, I had a belief system but no power or desire to carry out the truths of Scripture. Even after my conversion experience at age fifteen, I came to the conclusion that there had to be more. I think all of us have had that thought from time to time—the sense that there has to be more to our Christian life.

If you're like me, you probably never pursued that thought for long, out of fear of where it might lead. Although I knew there had to be more, I honestly was afraid to go for God's best, to pursue all he had to offer me—particularly when it came to opening myself up to the Holy Spirit. The possibilities seemed incredibly dangerous. In fact, I thought if I really sold out to God, I'd spend the rest of my life as a missionary living in a mud hut in the African bush. I thought I'd be required to go door-to-door and warn people to turn or burn. And if that's what it meant to be 100 percent sold out to God, I was just fine getting by with what I had. It seemed safer to have just enough God to get to heaven, but not so much that he radically altered my life.

But my frustrations continued. It was literally like having everything I needed within sight but no way to grab hold of it. I felt like I'd been given the keys to a new car with no gas in the tank.

Eventually, a friend of mine invited me to a small group meeting where they began talking about the power of the Holy Spirit. Immediately, my defenses went up and all my fears about that church fight when I was a kid came rushing back. But at the same time, everything in me wanted more, wanted to let go of the old ideas and recycled rumors, and to find out for myself what the Spirit was really all about.

So I opened my heart to him. All I can say is that it changed everything for the better. I went from being a weak, milk-fed Christian to a radical, on-fire believer who couldn't stop reading my Bible and inserting Christ into conversations with my friends. And the best part? I wasn't trying to be a "good Christian"! I was just being myself and allowing the Spirit into my heart, my mind, my life. I surrendered all I'd heard about the Spirit so I could experience the adventure of God's presence in my life firsthand.

BOLD AND UNASHAMED

The Bible clearly shows us that the disciple Peter was very close to Jesus. And I guess after being a friend and disciple for three years, Peter should've known Jesus better than most people. Yet when Jesus was arrested and standing trial before the Jewish leaders, Peter was still so weak in his faith that he denied being associated with or even aware of Christ. He did this not once, but three times—right after declaring undying loyalty to his Master. At a time when Jesus needed him most, Peter had no power to support or encourage him.

Of course, Peter's story doesn't end there. Fifty days after Jesus gave his life and was resurrected from the dead, Peter and over one hundred others encountered the Holy Spirit in a life-changing, breath-giving way that forever altered their lives. Within a matter of weeks, this same Peter, who had been ashamed to tell one slave girl that he knew Jesus, was preaching the message of the gospel in front of thousands. Even when Peter was arrested, he remained totally bold and unashamed of his relationship with Jesus.

What happened on that fiftieth day that hadn't happened

during those previous three years? It was this: Peter received supernatural power, God's breath, the confident life force of faith, and it made all the difference. How can we have a similar experience, a life-giving encounter with the breath-blast of God?

If you're like a lot of people, especially those raised in church, you may have some misconceptions, maybe even some biases, that make it difficult for you to get close to the person of the Holy Spirit. Most of us understand God the Father. We get that one because we all have an earthly father. We know what a father is like or what a good father should be like.

It's pretty easy to understand Jesus the Son too. God with us in the flesh, Immanuel, came to earth as a baby in a manger, died as a sinless man on the cross, and returned to life as the radiant Son who made it possible for us to know his Father. Most of us have some understanding of Jesus because we've seen pictures and movies that depict him, even if they're not fully accurate.

But what's up with this Holy Ghost? If you're like I was for years, it may seem easier to stay away and avoid the topic altogether. We don't have a positive association with "ghosts" and all the spooky, supernatural mystery that surrounds them. That's the stuff of scary movies and Halloween stories, and it's best if those topics aren't brought into our everyday lives. But as I discovered, if we want to experience God's breath of fresh air in our lives, we must rethink our assumptions about the Holy Spirit.

BREAKING THE BARRIERS

If you spend much time reading Acts, it becomes clear that God didn't give us his Spirit as an option but as a necessity. The Holy

Spirit is our lifeline to the Father; he's the One who empowers us to become who we were created to be.

Notice the response Paul gets from some early Christians when he asks them about the Holy Spirit:

> While Apollos was at Corinth, Paul took the road through the interior and arrived at Ephesus. There he found some disciples and asked them, "Did you receive the Holy Spirit when you believed?" They answered, "No, we have not even heard that there is a Holy Spirit." (Acts 19:1–2)

Almost like a baby who hasn't yet discovered the voice she can use to speak, these early believers didn't realize what was available to them.

My fear is that a lot of us allow fear, misinformation, and ignorance of the truth to prevent us from relating to our Breath-Giver as well. Many people today have doctrinal beliefs but not biblical beliefs. Some have been told that the Holy Spirit does not operate today like he did as recorded in the Bible. Some believe that the Spirit's presence was a onetime, limited engagement for the early church, and that he's either unavailable or unnecessary for believers today. But the Bible never says that.

Some people have been turned off by those who claim to have a Spirit-filled life and are tired of being made to feel inferior, like second-class Christians, if they don't behave "in the Spirit" just like those people. Some people have been turned off by extreme expressions that are not even close to what the Bible describes.

What would it look like if we threw out all our biases? I call it the "fresh-page approach" to the Bible. What if we didn't bring in what religion, history, our past experiences, or other people have told us? What if we had no preconceived notions about the Holy Spirit? What if we were reading the Bible for the first time?

With this fresh approach, I'm convinced we would come to the conclusion that the Holy Spirit permeates the entire Bible. We'd see him in the Old Testament as he moved on the face of the earth during creation. We'd see how he empowered different people, such as David and Samson, for different tasks. We'd see that the prophet Joel prophesied that the Spirit would be poured out on all flesh and to all generations.

In the New Testament, we'd see how John the Baptist explained that the Messiah, Jesus, would baptize us in the Holy Spirit. We'd see how Jesus was anointed with the Holy Spirit, and as a result was empowered to heal and deliver those oppressed by the devil (as in Acts 10:38). We'd see how the Holy Spirit asked the early church (in Acts 13:1–3) to set aside Paul and Barnabas so they could embark on their first missionary journey. Finally, we'd conclude that the Spirit's role in the lives of believers is as vitally important today as it was two thousand years ago.

If we look carefully and comprehensively at the Scriptures, we see that the Holy Spirit is not a status symbol, not the be-all, end-all experience, not a scary presence to be avoided. We see that he's simply a friend unlike any other, one who can put the wind back in our sails. He's not a flimsy, ethereal, floating cloud without substantive presence in our lives. He's real. He's the ultimate rush of grace, the ultimate breath of fresh air.

HAVE WE MET?

For the next few minutes, I'd like to introduce you to the Holy Spirit in a more personal way. I encourage you to grab a piece of paper and pen or a keyboard so that you can jot down the things that might surprise you about who the Holy Spirit really is. As we've discussed, his identity is often mistaken and misunderstood, so it's important that we grasp who he is and the role he plays in our lives.[1]

The best place to begin, simply enough, is to remember that *the Holy Spirit is God*. In some instances, Scripture uses the names *God* and *Spirit* interchangeably or indicates their unique trinitarian relationship. "Then Peter said, 'Ananias, how is it that Satan has so filled your heart that you have lied to the Holy Spirit? . . . You have not lied just to human beings but to God'" (Acts 5:3–4). By lying to the Spirit, Ananias lied to God himself.

Or consider this example: "Go and make disciples of all nations, baptizing them in the name of the Father and of the Son and of the Holy Spirit" (Matthew 28:19). So if you ever hear someone say, "Watch out for that Holy Spirit church over there!" keep in mind that they're actually saying, "Watch out for that God church over there!"

Next, we must realize that *the Holy Spirit is an actual person* and not an "it." When we interact with the Holy Spirit, we're relating to a person, not catching a cold or the flu. I know it may be bad grammar, but *he* is a *him*, and it's so important that we see the Spirit as a person—not human, but still with what we think of as a personality. The Bible never refers to the Spirit as "it" but always as "him." If we don't see the Spirit as someone we can relate to and get to know, it remains tough for us to have an intimate relationship with him.

Consider Jesus's words to his disciples about the Spirit of truth:

> The world cannot accept *him*, because it neither sees *him* nor knows *him*. But you know *him*, for *he* lives with you and will be in you. (John 14:17)

Don't miss it. The Holy Spirit is a person who wants to relate to us personally.

It's also important to dispel any notions that he's odd or peculiar. *The Holy Spirit is not weird,* though sometimes people are. They may distort things and try to use the Spirit to justify their behaviors. He won't tell women not to wear any makeup. And he won't make them wear too much makeup either. He won't make you line dance down the church aisles or laugh uncontrollably at your pastor's jokes (unless they're really funny). Seriously, I'm tired of people talking about the Spirit the way they do. Satan has lied to us about him and given him a bad rap. We've become afraid and distanced from the One whom God intends to be our lifeline.

Our enemy knows that if we all embrace the Spirit and access his power in our lives, we'll experience unprecedented revival, healing, and reconciliation. We'll become like the church described in Acts where thousands discovered Christ and hundreds were healed in his name, all in one day.

In fact, Jesus said that the Spirit is so powerful that it would be best for the disciples that Jesus leave them so they could receive the Holy Spirit: "But very truly I tell you, it is for your good that I am going away. Unless I go away, the Advocate will not come to you; but if I go, I will send him to you" (John 16:7).

Finally, *the Holy Spirit is our best friend.* If you've ever had a truly close friend, you know how comfortable it is to be able to relax and be yourself around him or her. That's what the Holy Spirit wants us to do around him. He's an encourager and a comforter, a protector and an uplifter unlike any other we'll ever have. He knows and wants what is best for us. "The amazing grace of the Master, Jesus Christ, the extravagant love of God, the intimate friendship of the Holy Spirit, be with all of you" (2 Corinthians

13:14 MSG). We need to be in relationship with the Father, Son, and Holy Spirit and receive the special gifts that each offers us.

Notice that Paul's beautiful benediction above begins with Jesus. It all starts there. Our relationship with him is unique because Jesus gives us grace so that we may be forgiven of our sins. What Jesus did for us we could never do for ourselves. When we receive Jesus's grace, when we accept the gift that he gave on the cross, we can begin to experience the extravagant love of the Father.

But many people forget about the daily intimate friendship with the Holy Spirit that is ours once we come to Christ. Yet we need him as our friend every day—to remain connected to God, to talk to him, to feel his presence, and to experience his power.

MY BEST FRIEND

Our relationship with the Holy Spirit is a unique friendship. To find clarity about the Spirit's role in our lives, I went to John 14–16, a record of one of Jesus's final messages, in which he introduces us to the Spirit and reveals how his presence enriches our lives in every way. Jesus says, "I will ask the Father, and he will give you another advocate to help you and be with you forever" (John 14:16). The Greek word here for advocate (or "counselor," in some versions) is *parakaleo*, literally "one called alongside to help." Some Bible commentaries point out that the same word refers to someone who picks up the other end of the log you're carrying. I love this image of the Spirit being a very practical helper and co-laborer in our lives.

Parakaleo can also be translated as "comforter," one who lightens your burdens through encouragement and instruction. In fact, one of the most practical benefits of the Holy Spirit is the way he teaches us. "But the Advocate, the Holy Spirit, whom the Father will send in my name, will teach you all things and will remind you of everything I have said to you" (John 14:26). The Holy Spirit is the author of the Bible. He inspired and directed the writing of each book. He knows how to bring each verse into our everyday lives. He will reveal the truths of Scripture to you when you listen. For this reason, I always keep a pad of paper handy when I'm reading God's Word so that I can journal or take notes. The Spirit always seems to inspire thoughts, questions, new connections, and applications. He loves to teach us; after all, he is the source of revelation and the power that enables Scripture to begin working in us.

GET THE MESSAGE

The Holy Spirit also helps us share the Good News of Christ with those around us. "When the Advocate comes, whom I will send to you from the Father—the Spirit of truth who goes out from the Father—he will testify about me" (John 15:26). Sharing the gospel message is at the heart of the Spirit's purpose. So many people have tried to make the Spirit's purpose something other than what it is, which is to reveal Jesus to us and help us reveal Jesus to others. In Acts 2, what was the first thing that happened on the day of Pentecost after the Spirit showed up? Three thousand people received Jesus into their lives.

When he fills us, the Spirit enables us to be more effective in reaching people. The Holy Spirit's job is to give us the words to speak as we witness. We may be timid and afraid to testify about Christ, but we find our voice naturally when we allow the Spirit to inspire us and lead us. "You will receive power when the Holy

Spirit comes on you; and you will be my witnesses in Jerusalem, and in all Judea and Samaria, and to the ends of the earth" (Acts 1:8).

Many times I get an impression about someone's life—the struggle or relational challenge he or she is facing—and I feel compelled to share Christ with that person. I remember watching a server in a restaurant and sensing that she was probably having to work several jobs to make ends meet. I left a very large tip and made it a point to tell her that God cared about her. Grateful for my generosity, she told me how she was juggling multiple jobs and how much my tip and prayers meant to her. I left the restaurant knowing the Holy Spirit had been guiding me in that encounter.

The Spirit will also convict us of sin in our lives. He reveals our true condition to us, not in a way that condemns us, but in a way that helps us admit the truth and remain connected to God by confessing and embracing his forgiveness. He gently stirs our consciences and makes us aware of what is true and what will please our Father.

Jesus said, "Unless I go away, the Advocate will not come to you; but if I go, I will send him to you. When he comes, he will prove the world to be in the wrong about sin and righteousness and judgment" (John 16:7–8). The Holy Spirit's role is to put the spotlight on areas of our lives where sin hides in dark corners. You know, those places where we try to justify our selfish choices or deny the real problems. He reminds us of our new nature—Christ's righteousness—and focuses us back to our priorities, our eternal concerns for God's kingdom. "Whether you turn to the right or to the left, your ears will hear a voice behind you, saying, 'This is the way; walk in it'" (Isaiah 30:21).

Unlike Satan, who is constantly condemning us, the Spirit gently redirects us to something better than the tempting but destructive allure of sin.

Even when we yield to temptation, the Spirit not only convicts us, he also will guide us through the many twists and turns of our lives, always reminding us of God's wisdom. "When he, the Spirit of truth, comes, he will guide you into all truth" (John 16:13). When we want direction in our lives and guidance about certain decisions, when we want to know God's will for our lives, we need to turn to the Holy Spirit. The Holy Spirit will give us an inward voice and witness, showing us the right decisions to make. He will guide us into the right direction in all our decisions. We can follow him and have inward peace.

I was reminded of how true that is just before Church of the Highlands launched in 2001. After much prayer and searching, our launch team had found what appeared to be a great location in which to meet. Then one day as I was driving down the highway, I was sure I heard the Holy Spirit say, "Don't launch there."

I called a member of our team who was surprised when I told him this, but like me he felt we had to follow the Spirit's prompting. Three days later, we met with the principal of an area high school who enthusiastically showed us around his building and predicted that we would quickly fill the auditorium. The team was convinced this was the place God was leading us.

Once back at my office, I knew I needed to call the manager of the other facility and ask if we could be released from our contract. I needn't have worried. As soon as I told her of our desire to meet elsewhere, she said, "I'm kind of glad. I was afraid you were going to break everything around this place. I'll talk to you later." Boy, was I glad I listened to the Holy Spirit! Launching a church is difficult enough without meeting at a facility where you're not really welcomed.

There's nothing spooky, weird, or fuzzy about the Holy Spirit.

He's God, he's in your life, and he's your friend. If you're stuck in the doldrums and don't know how to move forward, the Spirit is the ultimate wind in your sails. He is God's blast of breath inside you, empowering you and guiding you to your truest self and your most abundant life. If you want fresh air in your life, let him be your friend. It's that simple.

BREATHING LESSON

As we've explored, there are a lot of misconceptions about the Holy Spirit and his role in our lives. If you want to experience a breath of fresh air in your life, you must be connected to him as your power source. While this may seem daunting or even a little scary based on your past experiences or what you've heard, I encourage you to set aside some time to pursue further who the Holy Spirit is and what his role in our lives should be.

Begin by setting aside your biases so you can start your investigation with a blank page. You might meditate on passages of Scripture related to who the Spirit is, or read other books that explore this even more. If you ask him, he will lead you to know him at a deeper, more intimate level of friendship.

> You will call on me and come and pray to me, and I will listen to you. You will seek me and find me when you seek me with all your heart.
>
> —Jeremiah 29:12–13

14

TAKE A DEEP BREATH

Follow the river and you will find the sea.

FRENCH PROVERB

Several years ago, some buddies and I decided to watch the movie *The Bucket List*. I'm not a big film fan, so my expectations weren't very high. But to my surprise, God used the movie as a turning point in my life. *The Bucket List* tells the story of two men from very different backgrounds who meet as patients in a cancer ward. They eventually become friends and together make a list of things they want to do before they "kick the bucket."

If you've seen the movie, you know the wonderful message that hides just beneath the humor: All the thrills in the world can't satisfy the soul like a few eternal intangibles. Things like relationships, laughter, and living in a way that makes a positive difference. Moments of beauty and exhilaration that come from sharing experiences together with people you love. Setting goals and taking risks. Enjoying life *right now, today.*

God used the movie to inspire me. At forty-four, I realized I was at my "halfway" point and no longer dreamed of exciting adventures in the future. I was maintaining the status quo—a good marriage, five good kids, and a good church. But now I set a goal to make my own list of things I wanted to do before I kicked the bucket.

Creating my list's first draft was more fun than I expected. I quickly jotted down twenty-five items at random, including:

Celebrate an anniversary in Italy.
Take a pilgrimage to the Holy Land.
Build a world-class ministry college.
Fly in an F-16 jet.
Plant two thousand churches in America and around the world.
Play a round of golf at Augusta National Golf Club.
Write a book (that people actually want to read).
Go to every Major League Baseball park with one of my four boys.

I was amazed how this little exercise stirred in me a driving passion to live a richer life—one full of the breath of God. I realized that complacency in any area of my life would quickly lead to a life void of purpose and meaning, with no wind, no breath. That's not what I wanted in my life's second half. I wanted more, and I knew God longed to give me more than what I'd settled for in middle age. Since starting this practice, I've continued to cross off items on my bucket list and to update it with new goals, hopes, and dreams.

Whatever our age or current season of life, the same thing is true for all of us: If we stop growing and settle into a maintenance-and-survival mode, we'll eventually become stagnant.

During my nearly thirty years of ministry, I've seen so many Christians just coasting through life. They've been in church for a long time, so long that at any given moment of a church service, they can predict what will happen next. It almost becomes a game for them—you can sense them quietly challenging the pastor or teacher: *You can't surprise me. Been there, heard that a dozen times.*

Some Christians have gone through the routine for so long that their faith has become stale, bland, and impotent. That's a dangerous place to be. The enemy capitalizes on our complacency to keep us immature, never enjoying God's breath of fresh air. As this book concludes, I want to inspire you to pursue all that God has for you. I want to encourage you to open your heart to a fresh revelation from God, to pursue the Holy Spirit and let him fill your life with fresh air. I want to challenge you to climb to higher heights.

BEYOND YOUR IMAGINATION

How would you complete this sentence: "God is . . ." Most people answer with something they've already discovered about him: "God is my peace, my healer, my protector, my provider." The statements are all true, but these and a thousand more would still not define God—because God is more than we could ever grasp, let alone define. If you said, "God is faithful," he's still more faithful than you could possibly imagine. If you said, "God is loving," you still haven't come close to comprehending how abundant his love is.

Here's what I've discovered: God is not limited to what we're currently experiencing or how we've known him in the past. How depressing would it be if God were only what you've already discovered and nothing more? He is more than you or I could ever dream or imagine. God "is able to do immeasurably more than all we ask or imagine" (Ephesians 3:20).

Could it be that we've settled with our current understanding and experience of God? In our relationship with God have we gravitated to an incredibly safe lifestyle? Are we serving God but attempting to stay in control of our own lives? Is our faith so predictable and uninspiring that we're bored and stagnant?

Maybe it's time to do something drastically different. To take God at his word, even when it feels uncomfortable or vulnerable or unfamiliar. To let go of the past and pursue his Spirit and breath like never before. If he is the God who can and will do exceedingly and abundantly more than all we could ask, imagine, or think, why not let him? What will it take for us to let God saturate our lives with his love and resuscitate our hearts with his life-giving breath?

OUT OF CONTROL

Here's something I know about God and the Christian walk: God will always require the big leap from us—a step of faith. When we step out by faith, we don't know what's ahead of us. We walk on God's path and can't see what's around the bend. We may not like this uncertainty and lack of control, but the Bible is clear: Without faith it's impossible to please God (as we read in Hebrews 11:6). He rewards those who diligently and earnestly pursue him.

Even when I knew I was genuinely saved and pursuing all God had for me, I remained guarded. I was sure there had to be more to the Christian life but was afraid to go there because of my preconceived notions. The first time I invited the Holy Spirit to fill me, my prayer was a mixed bag of double messages—something like this: "Holy Spirit, I want to receive you, but at the same time I don't want to lose control. I want you to come in on my terms. I'll receive you, but I still have some concerns about you and your ways. If you can behave yourself, you're welcome to come in and stay awhile."

It sounds like a halfhearted contract with an unruly tenant instead of a commitment of love and spiritual adventure with the God of the universe. I can laugh about it now, mostly because later I became convicted about how lukewarm I was being. Like so many people, I'd let my religious prejudices taint my beliefs and color my perceptions. Finally, though, I said, "I want you and everything you have to offer—all of me for all of you."

I was learning at last the importance of not holding back, of going all in. "You will seek me and find me when you seek me with all your heart" (Jeremiah 29:13). It can't be halfway. It can't be someday. It can't be just enough to get by on. It must be total, wholehearted, and beyond your control.

On Easter Sunday 2012, over three thousand people came to Christ at our church's various campuses. In the book of Acts, we see that the first Christians were always baptized immediately after they came to faith, and our team felt that was an important step for these new believers to take as well. So the Sunday after Easter, Highlands held a spontaneous baptism service.

Audrey (whom you met earlier) was there that Sunday with her husband, kids, and her parents. In her blog post, she describes her reaction when I announced this service:

> This week, Pastor Chris surprised us all by doing an impromptu baptismal service! An opportunity for all those recently saved

> and anyone else who has not been baptized yet to be baptized today during the service! *What??* And he left no room for excuses. They had complete changes of clothes for anyone of any size who wanted to get baptized . . . shorts, T-shirts, and, yes—even undergarments! They even had ponytail holders, blow dryers, and hair mousse for those who needed it.
>
> My daughter turned to me with tears in her eyes. . . . I asked, "Are you doing it?" She eagerly nodded yes as tears filled up her eyes and she wrapped her arms around my neck for a good long squeeze as we both cried together. Then I turned to Chris (my hubby who became a Christ follower 4.5 years ago on Christmas Eve) and asked him if he was going to do it and he simply nodded his head and said, "Yeah!" Within the next 60 seconds they were both getting their T-shirt and shorts and got in line with so many others who decided to get baptized today. It was so awesome.

What I love about this story is the willingness of Audrey's husband and daughter to follow the Spirit's lead, to do something they hadn't planned on. As a result, her family was blessed in a way they will never forget. She ended her post this way:

> What made today even more special is that my parents happened to be in town to watch my son's baseball tournament and visited church with us for the first time this morning. We left church just beaming and filled with joy! What an amazing experience that we will never forget—what a *God* thing, ya know?

In addition to Audrey's husband and daughter, 1,107 people were baptized at Church of the Highlands that day.

ROLLING DOWN THE RIVER

About an hour northwest of our home in Birmingham is Smith Lake. For a place with such a generic-sounding name, it's one of the most amazing lakes in the country, with over five hundred miles of wooded shoreline around freshwater that's over two hundred feet deep in many spots. It's a wonderful place to play on the water, whether boating, fishing, skiing, or tubing. Smith Lake also features several rocky cliffs along its edges where courageous (or crazy) swimmers like to jump or dive.

The tallest cliff I'm aware of is about as high as a four-story building. When I first saw it, I realized that my common sense was stronger than either my ego or my back, and that I didn't have anything to prove by jumping. However, as I talked to one of my crazy friends who had to try it, he said, "You can't think about what you're doing—you just have to do it!" Sometimes I think this mindset is how we should approach our relationship with the Holy Spirit.

My friend's comment reminds me of a body of water mentioned by the prophet Ezekiel:

> As the man went eastward with a measuring line in his hand, he measured off a thousand cubits and then led me through water that was ankle-deep. He measured off another thousand cubits and led me through water that was knee-deep. He measured off another thousand and led me through water that was up to the waist. He measured off another thousand, but now it was a river that I could not cross, because the water had risen and was deep enough to swim in—a river that no one could cross. (Ezekiel 47:3–5)

This river gives us a great illustration of the way in which God calls us to let go of our attempts to control and find the place where he preserves and directs us. In the shallow water, we tend to feel in control since we can touch the bottom. But in the middle, God invites us to swim, to immerse ourselves in all that he has for us.

As Ezekiel discovers, the flowing waters in the middle of the river are life-giving, making the surrounding riverbanks especially fertile and beautiful. Where the river flows, everything will live:

> Fruit trees of all kinds will grow on both banks of the river. Their leaves will not wither, nor will their fruit fail. Every month they will bear fruit, because the water from the sanctuary flows to them. Their fruit will serve for food and their leaves for healing. (Ezekiel 47:12)

Ezekiel's revelation holds true for us today. Many of us prefer just to wade in the river, experiencing some of God's mystery while staying in control by keeping our feet firmly on the river bottom. Yet the Spirit of God invites us to go from ankle-deep faith to one that's knee-deep, then waist-deep, and finally to where we can no longer touch bottom at all—we're no longer in control of our own lives. We dive into the middle and swim in the powerful current of God's extravagant love and abundant joy.

So venture out from the bank. Go where your feet can't touch the bottom. Experience the exhilaration and adventure that come when you let the river take you wherever it flows.

JUST BREATHE

We began our journey in this book by looking at the doldrums and thinking about how it feels when we get stuck, and how much better it feels to experience a fresh breeze, a second wind, a breath of fresh air in our lives. We explored how we can reinvigorate our lives by developing habits and practices that make room for the breath to flow in all areas of our lives. And we focused on the Holy Spirit, the source of God's life-giving presence:.

We've come near the edge now—and it's time to jump in.

BREATHING LESSON

Many people are afraid to jump in because they want to stay in control. But the truth is that none of us can ultimately control our lives, nor do we really want to try. We long for the safety of our Father's arms and the intimate friendship of his Spirit. In the same way I put together a bucket list to challenge myself and invigorate my life, I dare you to go for what you long for most. I challenge you to put yourself on a spiritual growth adventure where you experience the breath of God's Spirit.

So what are the next steps? Open your heart to the Holy Spirit. His presence in our lives is a free gift, just like our salvation. Don't let fear keep you from a real relationship with the One who *is* breath and who also gives you breath. All you have to do is ask and receive—and get ready for life's most exciting adventure.

As you finish reading this page, I encourage you to still yourself for a moment and breathe deeply. Inhale and be aware of how the air fills your lungs and sends oxygen to all parts of your body. Exhale and release the breath that's no longer needed. You need air to live. If you don't breathe, you'll die. Spiritually, you need the life-giving air that God wants to breathe into each of us.

Take a deep breath and let him in.

> No one's ever seen or heard anything like this, never so much as imagined anything quite like it—what God has arranged for those who love him. But you've seen and heard it because God by his Spirit has brought it all out into the open before you. The Spirit, not content to flit around on the surface, dives into the depths of God, and brings out what God planned all along.
>
> —1 Corinthians 2:9–10 MSG

15

POWER SURGE

Trying to do the Lord's work in your own strength is the most confusing, exhausting, and tedious work of all. But when you are filled with the Holy Spirit, then the ministry of Jesus just flows out of you.

CORRIE TEN BOOM

When it comes to our relationship with the Holy Spirit, we often settle for an oxygen mask rather than a wind turbine. Instead of relying on the power of the Holy Spirit daily and hourly, I wonder if we wait to lean into him until we're facing a painful crisis, unexpected loss, or major disappointment. It reminds me of how we sometimes consider prayer a last resort instead of our first response.

Relationships require us to engage and to communicate, not wait until we're desperate because we're unable to go it alone. God makes it clear that he wants us to know him and experience intimacy within a loving relationship with him—not view him as a distant judge we're forced to grovel before when confronted with our limitations.

What would your life look like if you relied on the breath of the Holy Spirit—not as a life-support system, but as the source of supernatural power exceeding your own abilities?

That's the question I set out to answer in this book. I've wanted to describe what happens when we experience an ongoing spiritual breeze in our lives, a breath of fresh air that empowers us to be who God made us to be, which in turn allows us to be fresh air for everyone around us, a conduit for his love, goodness, and power. So many people had asked me about the secret sauce that characterizes Church of the Highlands and wanted the recipe that I felt compelled to share it. However, rather than a list of ingredients that can be assembled, combined, and cooked to produce the same results every time, I've tried to make it clear that you have to start with the chef. You have to begin with yourself and your relationship to the Creator.

God works with whatever we give him to produce his masterpiece in our lives. But when we're holding back—when we bounce between hot and cold toward God, and end up lukewarm—we miss out. We get in our own way and impede the process of being more of who he made us to be, and of experiencing and enjoying the adventure of abundant living. We get in a rut and lose sight of relating to God. We relegate him to the corner of our lives, reconnecting only on Sundays, or when our small group meets, or when we feel like praying and reading his Word.

The Holy Spirit is our comforter, confidant, and catalyst for growing closer to God. His power enables us to be better than we can be on our own. Being filled with his power doesn't make us better than other people—only better than who we are without him!

OPERATING INSTRUCTIONS

To experience the fullness of the Spirit's power in all aspects of your life, you have to go all in.

To better understand what this process of intentional surrender looks like, we gain insight by looking at Pentecost, the occasion when the gift of the Spirit first arrived. You'll recall that Jesus had promised this gift to his followers several times, both before and after his resurrection. During the forty-day period after rising from the tomb but prior to his ascending to heaven, Jesus appeared to his disciples many times. On one of these occasions, he gave these instructions:

> Do not leave Jerusalem, but wait for the gift my Father has promised, which you have heard me speak about. For John baptized with water, but in a few days you will be baptized with the Holy Spirit. (Acts 1:4–5)

Later—just before he was taken up into the clouds—Jesus gave them this promise:

> But you will receive power when the Holy Spirit comes on you; and you will be my witnesses in Jerusalem, and in all Judea and Samaria, and to the ends of the earth. (Acts 1:8)

Apparently, the disciples had some of the same questions you and I still ask about the Holy Spirit. They weren't exactly clear about how and when this gift would arrive, or about the kind of power it provided. Regarding the timing, Jesus replied that only the Father knew when the Spirit would arrive (1:7).

But the disciples didn't have to wait long—about ten days, based on the time markers referenced.

Scripture tells us that Jesus died during the Feast of Passover (John 19:31; Mark 15:42), then rose from the dead, then interacted with his followers for forty days (Acts 1:3) before ascending into heaven. According to the Jewish calendar of holy days, Pentecost was observed fifty days after the previous Passover, which leaves ten days between Christ's ascension and Pentecost.

The timing of these two major events of our faith—Jesus's death and resurrection at Passover, and the gift of the Holy Spirit at Pentecost—was no coincidence. Instead, it emphasizes once again the difference between the old ways of relating to God (through the law and external behavior) and the new personal and direct access we have through Christ. Passover commemorates God's deliverance of his people from bondage in Egypt, while Pentecost celebrates the way God provided for them during their forty-year trek to the Promised Land. Just as Jesus as the Lamb of God sacrificed himself for us at Passover, God's ultimate provision—His Spirit—arrived at Pentecost. And what a divinely dramatic entrance!

> When the day of Pentecost came, they were all together in one place. Suddenly a sound like the blowing of a violent wind came from heaven and filled the whole house where they were sitting. They saw what seemed to be tongues of fire that separated and came to rest on each of them. All of them were filled with the Holy Spirit and began to speak in other tongues as the Spirit enabled them. (Acts 2:1–4)

Some of those there that day struggled with understanding this gift—a problem many believers continue to wrestle with today. After receiving the gift of the Holy Spirit, as the followers of Jesus began to speak in other languages as evidence of his presence empowering them, the onlookers observing and listening weren't sure what was going on. "Amazed and perplexed, they asked one another, 'What does this mean?'" (Acts 2:12).

Their question reminds me of when our kids were little, and they'd open a Christmas or birthday present. Their eyes would widen with wonder and excitement at the new toy or game—until they opened the box and saw all the parts and pieces waiting to be assembled. They weren't sure how to put everything together in order to enjoy what they'd been given. This process required understanding the operating instructions.

Perhaps you can relate. I suspect that many Christians know they have the gift of the Spirit dwelling inside, but they aren't sure how to relate to this Person. As I mentioned previously, people have often been wary or afraid of the Holy Spirit's limitless power and divine unpredictability. Even after we've come a long way in our understanding—as I have, even since I first preached and taught these things about the Holy Spirit more than a decade ago—our relationship with him can continue to remain mysterious, vague, and unclear.

In the purest biblical sense, the gift of the Spirit is about *power*.

FROM "GOT TO" TO "GET TO"

I remember preaching on the Holy Spirit one Sunday and explaining the importance of Pentecost for us today. An older gentleman shook my hand afterward, and with a dazed look in his eyes asked, "So does this mean we're Pentecostal?"

I shouldn't have been surprised. His confusion reflects why I've never liked labels. They can be so subjective and create false assumptions and unnecessary barriers. The importance of Pentecost comes down to the power of the Holy Spirit in our lives. He basically empowers us to do three things that we simply cannot do on our own.

First, the Holy Spirit empowers us to live *righteously*.

You'll recall how the people in ages past related to God as described in the Old Testament. Because God gave human beings the freedom to choose, to live out of either the tree of life or the tree of the knowledge of good and evil, Adam and Eve chose to go their own way and disobey God. Their disobedience introduced sin into the world, altering the way future generations related to God. So he gave his people the law, concretely revealed when he gave the Ten Commandments to Moses on Mount Sinai.

The problem with obeying laws on stone, however, came down to our human tendency to yield to temptation and rebel against God. Simply put, the law was too hard to follow. We see this back-and-forth in how his people Israel related to God as again and again they first trusted and obeyed him, then rebelled and disobeyed him—repetitive cycles of idolatry and repentance.

Then Jesus came along and told us that he would write the law on our hearts. Instead of external tablets of stone, we internalize the law when we accept the free gift of salvation through Jesus's sacrifice on the cross. Once and for all, he paid the debt of sin that we couldn't pay. This shift makes a huge difference in how we relate to God!

Rather than living under the burden of performance and never pleasing God enough, we experience the freedom of being forgiven, being loved unconditionally, and being empowered for living the life of purpose God created us to enjoy. We can move from a mindset of "got to," and instead enjoy that we "get to" love and serve God in intimacy with him.

We may continue to struggle at times, but with the Holy Spirit dwelling inside us, our righteousness does not rely on us. Not on our behavior or effort, not on our hard work, and not on the amount of time we put in. "You, however, are not in the realm of flesh but are in the realm of the Spirit, *if indeed the Spirit of God lives in you*" (Romans 8:9).

Our righteousness comes from Christ. We're no longer defined by our past mistakes but by our present, eternal relationship with God through his Spirit. In this new freedom we discover our purpose and experience the joy of making a positive difference in the lives of others as we advance God's kingdom. We learn to follow the voice of the Spirit and trust his guidance: "Whether you turn to the right or to the left, your ears will hear a voice behind you, saying, "This is the way; walk in it" (Isaiah 30:21).

POWER TO CHANGE

When I think about the power of the Holy Spirit in action, moving us from our own ability to God's enabling, one of my favorite examples from Scripture is Simon Peter. Remember how boldly he preached after he received the Spirit at Pentecost? Even he might have wondered how he was able to speak so confidently and powerfully. Looking at the big picture of his life, we see such a transformation in Peter: from unassuming fisherman, to reckless and quick-tempered follower of Jesus, to bold and courageous leader of the early church. When we look at Peter's spiritual growth, the change we see should inspire us all with hope for the transformation taking place in our own lives.

Among all the disciples, Peter might seem unlikely to become the natural leader who immediately sees an opportunity on that day of Pentecost to share the message of Jesus and preach so powerfully. This is the same Peter who, only a few hours after claiming that he would always stick by his Master—and despite being told by Jesus what would actually happen—denied even knowing Jesus. And not once, not twice, but three times! If we fast-forward again to Pentecost, we see a Spirit-led, Spirit-fueled follower of Christ leading others to this new way of relating to God.

After the Holy Spirit descended on the followers of Jesus at Pentecost, they began speaking in a multitude of languages (Acts 2:4). We're told that many people came running to see the commotion, with some being astounded to hear their native language coming out of Jewish mouths. The impact was so dramatic that some accused these Spirit-filled believers of being drunk!

Peter jumped in and cleared up that misperception right away. He explained not only that they had not been drinking wine (at nine in the morning), but that they were filled with the Spirit of God. Peter started preaching. He penetrated the hearts of those listening with the good news of the gospel:

> Repent and be baptized every one of you in the name of Jesus Christ for the forgiveness of your sins, and you will receive the gift of the Holy Spirit. (Acts 2:38 ESV)

On that day of Pentecost, this uneducated, rough-around-the-edges fisherman delivered the very first Christian sermon with authority, passion, and clarity:

> And with many other words he bore witness and continued to exhort them. . . . So those who received his word were baptized, and there were added that day about three thousand souls. (Acts 2:40–41 ESV)

Yes, you read that correctly—*three thousand people* accepted Christ that day! This is the same Peter who just fifty days earlier couldn't even admit knowing Jesus when confronted by a girl, on the night before Christ's death. Now he was able to preach boldly and lead three thousand souls to the Lord. The power of the Holy Spirit enabled Peter to share the fresh air of the gospel message in ways likely beyond Peter's imagination.

SPIRITUAL DYNAMITE

Which brings us to the second way the Holy Spirit empowers us to live—*supernaturally.*

Considering this power in action can be troubling. It's a power that includes miracles and wonders and things beyond human capability and comprehension. We tend to want to control things. We even want to control the way God's Spirit works in us—which is not how he operates. Instead, the Holy Spirit will connect you to the realm God lives in, a dimension beyond our own that is literally *super*natural. This was seen also in how Jesus had lived:

> You know that God anointed Jesus of Nazareth with the Holy Spirit and with power. Then Jesus went around doing good and healing all who were oppressed by the devil, for God was with him. (Acts 10:38 NLT)

Why is living supernaturally so important? Because we face things that cannot be solved naturally. This spiritual power in action is critical. How else would people know whether Christianity is real? How else can they can discover that Jesus really was who he said he was—God's Son in human form?

Supernatural power is different from all others because it clearly and demonstrably changes lives and events in ways that are humanly (and often physically) impossible, as Paul showed:

> My message and my preaching were not with wise and persuasive words, but with a *demonstration of the Spirit's power*, so that your faith might not rest on men's wisdom, but on God's power. (1 Corinthians 2:4–5)

It's not up to us. It's not dependent on how skillfully we serve and lead, or how eloquent and smart we are. Because no matter how talented or gifted we may be, we're still human. Having the power of the Holy Spirit in us takes us to the next level by allowing us to be conduits of God's limitless, supernatural power.

When I consider this kind of supernatural power, I often think of dynamite. In fact, when the apostle Paul prayed for the believers at Ephesus to experience this kind of power, the word he used for it is from the Greek root word *dunamis*. That's the same word root that the inventor Alfred Nobel used to name his explosive chemical discovery. We also get the word *dynamic* from this root. But *dynamite* seems like a more accurate symbol for the power of the Holy Spirit.

Notice how many various ways Paul prays for these Ephesian Christians to be supercharged, explosive, and stronger than is humanly or naturally possible:

> I pray that from his glorious, unlimited resources he will empower you with inner strength through his Spirit. Then Christ will make his home in your hearts as you trust in him. Your roots will grow down into God's love and keep you strong. And may you have the power to understand, as all God's people should, how wide, how long, how high, and how deep his love is. May you experience the love of Christ, though it is too great to understand fully. Then you will be made complete with all the fullness of life and power that comes from God.
>
> Now all glory to God, who is able, through his mighty power at work within us, to accomplish infinitely more than we might ask or think. (Ephesians 3:16–20 NLT)

I can attest to experiencing the supernatural power of God in my life in ways that have no logical, rational, or natural explanation. When I look back across the years, there's abundant and recurrent evidence for how God did what seemed, felt, and *was* literally impossible in my life—all through his supernatural power at work. And it's not over yet!

You may recall that I got saved—radically saved—when I was fifteen. I loved God and had grown up in the church, but felt timid and powerless in relation to God, who I misperceived as some scary, angry old judge always wanting more from me. Then after I got saved and realized the Holy Spirit was now inside my heart, I started reading my Bible and learning just who he is and how he helps me.

With this basic understanding of the Holy Spirit, I opened my life to him—tentatively and cautiously at first, then gradually more and more. This included attending a small group (which felt like the scariest thing I could ever do at the time), then discovering a personal prayer language—something else that felt new and unfamiliar at first, but became more natural—or should I say supernatural—the more I engaged with knowing the Holy Spirit.

I remember being at summer camp at Paul B. Johnson State Park in Hattiesburg, Mississippi, and having one of the leaders pray prophetically over me. We were having a worship service in an outdoor arena, and this leader who had never met me came over and told me to lift my hands to God. This leader then prayed and told me that God would use me to reach many people, more than I could count, like the stars in the heavens. He said that praise and worship would be a hallmark of my ministry. The Spirit in me was already preparing and equipping me for what was ahead, and what I could not even imagine.

As I became more attuned to the voice of the Spirit, I knew I was called to serve in full-time ministry. This led my family and me to Colorado, where I served in youth ministry. A few years later, I felt led to make another big leap of faith. I'll never forget standing at a Barnes & Noble bookstore off the interstate outside of Birmingham, sipping my coffee and staring out the window at the busy traffic outside, and hearing the Spirit tell me to start a church there in Birmingham. It was the beginning of Church of the Highlands.

More recently, I marvel at how God's power has worked to actualize a Spirit-given dream of mine—to start a ministry college for training the next generations of servant leaders and pastors. While I had learned to expect the wonderfully unexpected from God, I still struggle to grasp how Highlands College came to life so beautifully and quickly, exceeding my imagination, which already held a Spirit-sized vision.

My dream began to crystalize more than a decade ago, and Highlands College was launched. Today it's an accredited four-year college known as "America's Ministry Leadership University," a reflection of its graduates who go out into the world and serve in virtually every ministry capacity imaginable. This next generation of servant leaders are receiving our holistic, four-pillar education in the classical model, focusing on academic instruction, ministry training, character formation, and spiritual development.

Our innovative, state-of-the-art campus spans seventy acres and features more than two dozen learning studios and classrooms, eight hands-on ministry training labs, a multistory residence hall and student apartments, multiple dining and recreation facilities, a fitness center, and an auditorium seating 1,300.

Please forgive me if I sound like I'm bragging or making a recruitment pitch. I simply don't know how to express my overwhelming excitement, enthusiasm, and expectation for how God will continue to grow and use Highlands College. I don't know how to fully attest to how God has orchestrated and synchronized and provided so much in his timing to accomplish what no human beings could on their own. I watched it happen, and I know the details of the story—and I still don't know how it came together!

And while our campus and buildings are both beautiful and functional, it's what you can't see—the doors miraculously opened, the provisions generously made, and the people amazingly assembled—that reflects God's power the most. There's no way Highlands College could exit, let alone be the stunning ministry training college it has become so quickly, without the supernatural power of the Holy Spirit behind it all.

MISSION ACCOMPLISHED

As I shared with you in this book's introduction, I've now made a transition to focus most of my time and energy on leading

Highlands College. While I remain founding pastor at Church of the Highlands, and I'm lovingly dedicated to serving it, the college has always held a special place in my heart, a love which has only grown since its inception. I say this not only to illustrate the Spirit's supernatural power in action, but also to emphasize the third way we're spiritually empowered—*to live on mission.*

God has put inside each of us a spiritual gift, a divinely designed custom purpose that utilizes all our abilities, talents, experiences, and passions. While living out our sacred purpose produces true contentment, joy, and satisfaction, our spiritual gifts make a life-giving difference in other people's lives. Signs and wonders, gifts and miracles, are not for our entertainment or to draw attention to ourselves. They reflect God's goodness, power, and glory as he uses us to fulfill his mission.

And it's going to take signs and wonders and miracles to accomplish your mission. Because you can never fulfill your God-given mission in your own power. What God designed you to do can be accomplished *only* as you rely on his power through his Spirit within you. As Paul once testified, "Our gospel came to you not simply with words but also with power, with the Holy Spirit and deep conviction" (1 Thessalonians 1:5).

As you consider the power available to you through God's Spirit within, I hope you will want more than you've experienced so far, regardless of whether that's been a little or a lot. I sometimes wonder if we limit how God wants to work through us by failing to dream big enough and to risk often enough. We hesitate to go all in on how God wants to use us to do amazing, mind-boggling, heart-thrilling, seemingly impossible things that presently exceed our imagination.

If I've learned one thing from my more than forty years with the Holy Spirit, it's to rely on his power to be all that God made me to be. When I consider how God has worked in my life and worked through me for his purposes, sometimes I just smile and shake my head. There's simply no way I could have accomplished any of those things on my own. And he's not through with me yet. For all I know, God might just be getting started!

The same is true for you. No matter where you are, regardless of your age and stage of life, there is always more fresh air, through the power of the Spirit, to revive and refresh you and also to help you bring spiritual fresh air to those around you.

Don't settle for an oxygen mask when you can have a wind turbine.

Don't slip back into old default fears, false assumptions, and misconceptions about the Holy Spirit. While prayer and Bible study are essential, spend some time in solitude with the Lord and reflect on what's been holding you back. Have an honest, heart-to-heart conversation with the Holy Spirit.

Now is the time to go all in—again. Cultivate your friendship with God's Spirit daily, acknowledging and embracing his presence in you, with you, and through you.

When you find yourself drifting back into the doldrums, when you feel stuck in one place, spend time reconnecting with the Spirit in you. There's nothing to be afraid of, and everything to be excited about.

Take a deep breath of the fresh air that's always available to you!

BREATHING LESSON

What do you still find confusing, unsettling, or troubling about your relationship with the Holy Spirit? How can you move through and beyond these obstacles in order to surrender yourself and your life to the full power of God's Spirit?

What's keeping you from experiencing the supernatural dynamite available to you through the Holy Spirit in your life?

My prayer for you is that you will rely singularly and wholeheartedly on the Spirit of God within you, the ultimate breath of fresh air. I pray that you will grow in peace, passion, and purpose as you experience more power of the Spirit in all areas of your life.

Allow yourself to fulfill the divine mission God has for you—and get ready to see him surprise and delight you again and again.

Amen.

> Now the Lord is the Spirit, and where the Spirit of the Lord is, there is freedom. And we all, who with unveiled faces contemplate the Lord's glory, are being transformed into his image with ever-increasing glory, which comes from the Lord, who is the Spirit.
>
> —2 Corinthians 3:17–18

ABOUT THE AUTHOR

Chris Hodges is the founding pastor of Church of the Highlands. Since it began in 2001 in Birmingham, Alabama, Highlands has grown to have campuses across the states of Alabama and Georgia.

Pastor Chris has a deep passion for developing leaders and planting life-giving churches. He co-founded ARC (Association of Related Churches) in 2001, which has launched hundreds of churches across the United States. He also founded GrowLeader, specializing in training and resourcing pastors and churches to help them break barriers and reach their growth potential. Chris is also the founder and chancellor of Highlands College, a ministry training school that trains and launches students into full-time ministry careers.

Chris and his wife Tammy have five children and live in Birmingham. He speaks at conferences worldwide. His prior books include *Fresh Air*, *Four Cups*, *The Daniel Dilemma*, *What's Next?*, *Out of the Cave*, and *Pray First*.

NOTES

CHAPTER 2

1. Audrey Curran is a lifestyle photographer who blogs at http://www.audreycurranblog.com.

CHAPTER 6

1. See http://www.uky.edu/Ag/AnimalSciences/dairy/extension/nut00014.pdf.
2. I am indebted to Rick Warren for first introducing me to these three principles.
3. Barna Group, "Barna Survey Examines Changes in Worldview among Christians over the Past 13 Years," March 6, 2009, http://www.barna.org/barna-update/article/21-transformation/252-barna-survey-examines-changes-in-worldview-among-christians-over-the-past-13-years. In addition to the validity of Scripture, respondents determined to hold a biblical worldview also agreed to the following: absolute moral truth exists; Satan is a real being or force, not merely symbolic; a person cannot earn their way into heaven by trying to be good or do good works; Jesus Christ lived a sinless life on earth; and God is the all-knowing, all-powerful creator of the world who still rules the universe today. In the research, anyone who held all of those beliefs was said to have a biblical worldview.

CHAPTER 8

1. Gary Chapman, *The 5 Love Languages: The Secret to Love That Lasts* (Chicago: Northfield Publishing, 1992).

2. The comments I made on this verse originated from a message I heard Rick Warren give.

CHAPTER 9

1. John Maxwell, *The 17 Indisputable Laws of Teamwork: Embrace Them and Empower Your Team* (Nashville: Thomas Nelson, 2001), xiv.
2. Charles Swindoll, *Day by Day with Charles Swindoll* (Nashville: Thomas Nelson, 2000), 242.
3. Gary Portnoy and Judy Hart Angelo, "Where Everybody Knows Your Name," 1982.

CHAPTER 10

1. We are a founding member of the Association of Related Churches, which by the end of 2012 will have planted nearly 350 churches.
2. Associated Press, "Consumer Borrowing Soared in November," *New York Times*, January 10, 2012.
3. See Richard A. Swenson, *Margin: Restoring Emotional, Physical, Financial, and Time Reserves to Overloaded Lives* (Colorado Springs, CO: NavPress, 2004), 42.

CHAPTER 11

1. If you'd like additional practical ideas on how to incorporate rest into your life, I recommend the book *Leading on Empty: Refilling Your Tank and Renewing Your Passion* by Wayne Cordeiro (Bloomington, MN: Bethany House, 2009).

CHAPTER 12

1. C. G. Finney, *Autobiography of Charles G. Finney: A Lifetime of Evangelical Preaching to Christians Across America, Revealed* (Minneapolis: Bethany, 1876, reprinted 1977), 21–22.

CHAPTER 13

1. Robert Morris first introduced me to these concepts.